Who Should Read This Book

This book is is not just for Jewish people. It is for all people who seek inspiration, strength to change, and spiritual renewal from Jewish tradition, especially those who are codependent.

✓ Anyone who is looking for a deepened understanding of the Twelve Steps from a Jewish perspective—regardless of religious background or affiliation

✓ Codependent people—fathers, mothers, sisters, brothers, husbands, wives, grandparents, lovers, coworkers, and friends: All people who are in a relationship with an alcoholic or addicted person, those in trouble with food, gambling, or sexual addictions or psychological dysfunction

- Jewish people: Reform, Conservative, Reconstructionist, Orthodox, unaffiliated

- All Jews who seek guidance and inspiration from a shared and sacred tradition

- People of all faiths who seek guidance, strength, and spiritual renewal through recovery

- Anyone who was raised in a dysfunctional family

- Adult children of alcoholics

✓ Friends who care

✓ Caregivers who help people in recovery

✓ Rabbis, priests, ministers, and spiritual counselors of all kinds

✓ Alcohol and chemical dependency counselors

✓ Psychiatrists, psychologists, therapists

✓ All people who have read *Twelve Jewish Steps to Recovery: A Personal Guide for Turning from Alcoholism and Other Addictions* (Jewish Lights Publishing, Woodstock, VT, 1991) and *Renewed Each Day: Daily Twelve Step Recovery Meditations Based on the Bible* (Jewish Lights Publishing, Woodstock, VT, 1992).

There are Twelve Gates in heaven symbolic of the Twelve Tribes. Each person's prayer goes up through one of those gates.

Isaac Luria, the *Ari Hakadosh*

Foreword by
Marc Galanter, M.D.,
Director, Division of Alcoholism and Drug Abuse,
New York University Medical Center

Afterword by
Harriet Rossetto,
Director, Gateways Beit T'shuvah

Recovery from

Codependence

A Jewish Twelve Steps Guide to Healing Your Soul

You may be a codependent person if you are in a relationship with an alcoholic or addicted person, someone who has an eating disorder, engages in compulsive gambling or sex, if you are addicted to a relationship, or if you are part of a dysfunctional family.

Rabbi Kerry M. Olitzky

JEWISH LIGHTS Publishing
Woodstock, Vermont

Recovery from Codependence: A Jewish Twelve Steps Guide to Healing Your Soul
copyright ©1993 by Kerry M. Olitzky

Library of Congress Cataloging-in-Publication Data

Olitzky, Kerry M., 1954–
Recovery from codependence: a Jewish twelve steps guide to healing your soul/Kerry M. Olitzky.
     p.   cm.
ISBN 1-879045-27-3 (cloth)—ISBN 1-879045-32-X (paper)
1. Twelve-step programs—Religious aspects—Judaism.
2. Codependency—Religious aspects—Judaism. 3. Compulsive behavior—Religious aspects—Judaism. I. Title.

BM538.T85044 1993
296.7'4—dc20   93–20051
                                                    CIP

First edition

10 9 8 7 6 5 4 3 2 1

Manufactured in the United States of America

Cover design by Lisa Ritter

Illustrations by Maty Grünberg

Published by JEWISH LIGHTS Publishing
A Division of LongHill Partners, Inc.
P.O. Box 237
Sunset Farm Offices, Route 4
Woodstock, Vermont 05091
Tel: (802) 457-4000
Fax: (802) 457-4004

For Earl and Joshua

Contents

CONTENTS

How to Use This Book

Like the Jewish Twelve Step books that have come before it, this book requires a special kind of reading. It's not the kind of book that you must sit and read cover to cover—but you may want to do just that. This book is designed for you, to meet your needs, for you to read a little or a lot at a time. It is designed to be read over and over again, accompanying you on your journey through recovery and spiritual renewal.

Read one step a day or one step a week or one step a month. Do whatever works for you. Just keep reading it. Together with Judaism and the Twelve Steps we can all find strength to heal and be renewed.

Kol Adonai bakoach. All persons hear God according to their own strengths, life experiences, and ability to hear. Torah and the Twelve Steps—as understood in a Jewish context taking us from being codependent to reaffirming our covenant with God—give us the strength to hear God's voice speak to us.

Acknowledgments

My contribution to this book is only as a spokesperson, giving voice to the dozens of people who have really written it, some without even knowing it. I merely put their words on paper. To the many who willingly poured out their hearts, sharing their souls, I thank them all—respectful of their desire to remain anonymous. Others permit mention by name. In particular, thanks to Arlene Chernow, who read and reacted to each word, opening her home and her family's life so that we might all heal together.

My friends at the JACS (Jewish Alcoholics, Chemically Dependent and Significant Others) Foundation continue to support this work, always there to help whenever I call. I mention specifically David Buchholz and Tami Crystal. I remain constantly indebted to them.

To my friends and colleagues at Hebrew Union College-Jewish Institute of Religion, thanks alone are never sufficient. There, I am provided with the supportive environment and nurturing that allows me to work and study—a privilege which I highly cherish. To Alfred Gottschalk, president; Paul Steinberg, vice president; and Norman Cohen, dean, I offer my most profound gratitude.

The folks at Jewish Lights have made their mark on Jewish history in a few short years. I feel privileged to work together with them. Stuart and Antoinette Matlins are really special people with whom I spend some of the most spiritually significant days of my religious life. To Rachel Kahn, whose wonderful skill as a designer of beautiful books helps people see the message, and

ACKNOWLEDGEMENTS

to Carol Gersten and Jay Rossier, who work so hard to help people know it is there to be seen, I express my thanks.

For my family, I offer a prayer of thanksgiving for every moment God has allowed us to spend time together on this fragile earth. *Hodu lAdonai kee tov; kee leolam chasdo.* "I acknowledge God's goodness to me, for God's loving acts are endless."

KERRY M. OLITZKY
New York, New York
Erev Rosh Hashanah 5753

Foreword

This is an unusual and useful book. It combines a sensitivity to the contemporary codependency movement with a thoughtful presentation of a related religious philosophy. The issue of codependency, namely the entwinement of people close to an addicted person with his or her compulsive behaviors, is one which has gained considerable public attention in recent years. It derives from the realization of many addicted people, as well as the health workers who serve them, that family members often contribute to perpetuating the dependency in alcoholics and drug abusers. This perspective has been closely associated with the growing popularity of Twelve Step movements like A.A. Its popularity illustrates the remarkable influence of a grass roots movement among those who affiliate, and their family members as well.

The spiritual orientation of A.A. itself can serve as an invaluable vehicle to achieving personal change. For this reason, members of this fellowship who are sensitive to their religious traditions can find positive change and facilitated understanding of the relationship between codependency and spiritual growth.

In order to understand the codependency concept we can first look at the background of Alcoholics Anonymous. The movement began in 1935 with Bill W., an accomplished financial analyst and an alcoholic. Bill had failed to stop drinking over the course of many hospitalizations. His resolve to change, which followed on the heels of an intense religious experience, led him to band together with other persons suffering the same malady so that they could work together as a group to stabilize their sobriety. The movement grew slowly in its initial years. As it became better known through the media, however, the great need for help with alcoholism, coupled by a paucity of treatment in the medical community, led to a burgeoning of membership. Today there are over one and a quarter million members of A.A. Importantly, the A.A. philosophy, as embodied in the Twelve Steps to recovery has become the operative philosophy of most alcoholism treatment programs in the United States. A.A. has legitimated the needs of the alcoholic person, supported the conception of alcoholism as a *bona fide* illness, and disseminated the conception of spirituality as a prime vehicle for recovery. Spirituality— and faith in a Higher Power as each alcoholic understands it—helps to give meaning to abstinence for a majority of Americans who seek help for their addictive problems.

Codependency did not emerge as a popular conception during the initial decades of A.A.'s history, although the concept was inherent in the development of Alanon. In order to help spouses and other relatives of alcoholics deal with their afflicted partners, A.A. members early on conceived of a movement that would provide those partners with the option of distancing themselves from the addict's behavior to give him or her the opportunity to move toward a decision to seek sobriety. It was conceived that the spouse did relatively little for the alcoholic by ministering to the needs generated by addiction and helped put off the time when he would come to the decision to seek appropriate help.

More recently the issue of codependency has been strengthened by a growing awareness of family systems theory which posits that a person's pathologic behavior is often the product of interactions with others, and does not necessarily or only reflect an inherent disability of his own. This conception can serve to relieve the alcoholic's guilt and thereby relieve him or her of a tendency to be defensively angry. Furthermore it can provide family members with an opportunity to seek an awareness of ways in which they may inadvertently contribute to perpetuating the addiction.

MARC GALANTER, M.D.
Director, Division of Alcoholism and Drug Abuse,
New York University Medical Center

What Is
Co-Dependents Anonymous?

*This material is reprinted from "Welcome to Co-Dependents Anony-
mous" with the permission of Co-Dependents Anonymous, Inc.
Permission to reprint does not mean that there is any affiliation
between Co-Dependents Anonymous and this book.*

Co-Dependents Anonymous is a fellowship of men and
women whose common problem is an inability to
maintain functional relationships.

We welcome you to Co-Dependents Anonymous a program of recovery from co-dependency where each of
us may share our experience, strength, hope in our
efforts to find freedom where there has been bondage
and peace where there has been turmoil in our relationships and our childhoods.

Most of us have been searching for ways to overcome
the dilemmas of the conflicts in our relationships and
our childhoods. Many of us were raised in families
where addictions existed—some of us were not. In
either case, we have found in each of our lives that codependency is a most deeply-rooted, compulsive
behavior and that it is born out of our sometimes mod-
erately, sometimes extremely dysfunctional family
systems.

We have each experienced in our own ways the painful
trauma of the emptiness of our childhood and relationships throughout our lives. We attempted to use
others—our mates, our friends, and even our children,

as our sole source of identity, value, and well-being and as a way of trying to restore within us the emotional losses from our childhoods. Our histories may include other powerful addictions which at times we have used to cope with our co-dependency.

We have all learned to survive life, but in CoDA we are learning to live life. Through applying the Twelve Steps and principles found in CoDA to our daily life and relationships, both present and past, we can experience a new freedom from our self-defeating lifestyles. It is an individual growth process. Each of us is growing at our own pace and will continue to do so as we remain open to God's will for us on a daily basis. Our sharing is our way of identification and helps us to free the emotional bonds of our past and the compulsive control of our present.

No matter how traumatic your past or despairing your present may seem, there is hope for a new day in the program of Co-Dependents Anonymous. No longer do you need to rely on others as a power greater than yourself. May you instead find here a new strength within to be that God intended—Precious and Free.

The Twelve Steps of Co-Dependents Anonymous

Reprinted and adapted with the permission of A.A. World Services, Inc. Reprinted with the permission of Co-Dependents Anonymous, Inc. Permission to reprint does not mean that there is any affiliation between Co-Dependents Anonymous and this book.

1. We admitted we were powerless over others—that our lives had become unmanageable.

2. Came to believe that a power greater than ourselves could restore us to sanity.

3. Made a decision to turn our will and our lives over to the care of God as we understood God.

4. Made a searching and fearless inventory of ourselves.

5. Admitted to God, to ourselves, and to another human being the exact nature of our wrongs.

6. Were entirely ready to have God remove all these defects of character.

7. Humbly asked God to remove our shortcomings.

8. Made a list of all persons we had harmed, and became willing to make amends to them all.

9. Made direct amends to such people wherever possible, except when to do so would injure them or others.

10. Continued to take personal inventory and when we were wrong, promptly admitted it.

11. Sought through prayer and meditation to improve our conscious contact with God as we understood God, praying only for the knowledge of God's will for us and the power to carry that out.

12. Having had a spiritual awakening as the result of these steps, we tried to carry this message to other co-dependents, and to practice these principles in all our affairs.

The Twelve Traditions
of
Co-Dependents Anonymous

1. Our common welfare should come first; personal recovery depends upon CoDA unity.

2. For our group purpose there is but one ultimate authority—a loving higher power as expressed to our group conscience. Our leaders are but trusted servants; they do not govern.

3. The only requirement for membership in CoDA is a desire for healthy and loving relationships.

4. Each group should be autonomous except in matters affecting other groups or CoDA as a whole.

5. Each group has but one primary purpose—to carry its message to other co-dependents who still suffer.

6. A CoDA group ought never endorse, finance or lend the CoDA name to any related facility or outside enterprise, lest problems of money, property and prestige divert us from our primary purpose.

7. Every CoDA group ought to be fully self-supporting, declining outside contributions.

8. Co-Dependents Anonymous should remain forever nonprofessional, but our service centers may employ special workers.

9. CoDA, as such, ought never be organized; but we may create service boards or committees directly responsible to those they serve.

10. CoDA has no opinion on outside issues; hence the CoDA name ought never be drawn into public controversy.

11. Our public relations policy is based on attraction rather than promotion; we need always maintain personal anonymity at the level of press, radio, and films.

12. Anonymity is the spiritual foundation of all our traditions, ever reminding us to place principles before personalities.

Letting Go

Step One

**WE ADMITTED
WE WERE POWERLESS OVER OTHERS—
THAT OUR LIVES HAD BECOME UNMANAGEABLE**

✓ The truth is often hard to admit. Sometimes, just speaking it helps to relieve us of its burden.

✓ All of us are powerless over one another, not just you and me.

✓ We can't concentrate on ourselves when our lives are a mess. It's our codependence that got us here.

We feel guilty, because we can't change the one we love. We suffer. The chaos and its pain eats away at us.

Power and control. A dangerous mix. They are the essential ingredients which lead us to a codependent relationship. A need to direct the lives of others overwhelms us. This is what might be described as "enabling behavior," the "passive stuff" we do that makes it easier for an addict to keep using, for an alcoholic to keep drinking, for a person with an eating disorder to keep bingeing. It drives us. We want people to be as we imagine them to be. In this futile pursuit and in the destructive relationship we may be trying to save, we lose ourselves. We feel guilty and then we get lost.

1

When a relationship is lost, even a bad one—whether it is to alcohol or drugs or overeating or gambling, sex or abusive behavior—we blame ourselves. Often, we repeat the same mistakes with other people. This cycle is a result of our codependence. Then when our repeated attempts at getting the other person to change, to give up drinking, using or abusing don't work—and they seldom do—we try to become another person.

To change the pattern of codependence, we do indeed have to become different people, but we must do so *to help ourselves,* not to change our husband or wife, sister or brother, mother or father, son or daughter, lover or friend. Our codependent other may continue to drown in active addiction, but we must swim to safety. We must change regardless of the impact of this change on the alcoholic or addict, the gambler or overeater.

It's this kind of "stinkin' thinkin'" that reinforces our codependence: Our assumption that, "If only I were _____ [any word will do], she would not act this way" is the kind of thinking leads us to conclude that it is *our* inadequacy that has forced the one we love away from us. It hurts. It hurts badly. And the pain creeps into the rest of our lives, affecting all that we are, all that we do—making us feel inadequate and of little self-worth. We fail, because we think we are a failure. We become the self-image we give ourselves.

This book will help you find strength to make changes in your life. Be prepared. The steps you will need to take may surprise you. Some may seem too simple, some too hard. You may think that they won't work.

That's OK. You're not alone. Plenty of other people felt the same way and they were helped and healed too. The steps will work—as long as you work them. You can count on it. They have worked for many others.

One codependent friend in recovery shared this experience with me: "I was taught that Jews didn't drink or drug. We were married young. I just always assumed that my husband started drinking because I was a terrible wife." The suffering, the hurt, and the anger that accompany codependence can consume you. Don't let it. Don't be angry at yourself, at your daughter, at her compulsive eating. Don't be hurt by your father's gambling. Hurt and anger will not pave the road to recovery and healthy, loving relationships. Instead, turn all that negative energy into spiritual strength and be renewed.

The time has come to move out of this paralysis, this codependence, to regain your true self. The road will be difficult, but you can see where it is that you have to travel. I won't kid you. The Israelites in their desert journey despaired. Every time you think that they finally "got it," that they were ready to give up on slavery and embrace freedom, leaving their old ways behind them, they soon were ready to run back to Egyptian servitude. They had forgotten how far they had come, the vast wilderness they had traversed. They were ready to give it all up. You may feel the same way.

Like the journey in the desert, the steps in recovery may be small and this first one probably will be the hardest. But once you have gotten started, you are well on your way.

To begin *this* journey, we have to acknowledge certain truths. First, we are unable to change others. We can only work to improve ourselves. Say it out loud. It helps to really hear what it is that we want to do.

Second, our lives have become unmanageable. And we are finally ready to take back control of our own lives. We are ready to move on to healthy and loving relationships. To do so, we have to evaluate the relationship with our codependent other—parent, child, spouse, sister, brother, lover, co-worker, friend. . . .

One father knew when it was time to admit his powerlessness. He told me, "I yell at her almost every morning. I repeat to her—word for word—the horrible things that she had said to me after I had waited up for her most of the night. It was then morning, and she'd had some sleep. Teary-eyed, she was filled with remorse. Feeling guilty, she left the house. Somehow because I yelled and she felt guilty, there was a sense that she had to change. Her all night partying—drinking and drugging—would stop. But I knew that the only way we could both take responsibility for our actions was when I stopped yelling."

Human relationships should mirror the covenant that God established with us at Sinai. It's what the philosopher Martin Buber called "I and Thou." It is a loving relationship of dialogue, of give and take. When one person is the only one giving and the other person is only taking, taking, taking—and you know what that's like—then the covenant is broken. There is no other way to say it. And that's no loving relationship. . . . That's codependence.

When Moses came down the mountain and saw that the Israelites had built a golden calf, he threw down the tablets of the covenant—the very core of the agreement—and they shattered. Later, Moses went back up the mountain and received a new set of instructions. The rabbis teach us that the Israelites gathered up these broken fragments, often cutting their hands to do so, and throughout their desert wanderings, carried the broken tablets in the ark of the covenant right next to the whole tablets. They were not to forget where the golden calf had led them. You shouldn't forget either. Memory reminds us of who we now are as much as who we once were. "There is no more central theme in Jewish self-perception than that of covenant," writes Rabbi Neil Gillman, contemporary theologian of the Conservative movement.

The Talmud tells us, "Great is the power of *teshuvah* [repentance, renewal], for it brings healing to the world. Even if only one person does *teshuvah,* both that individual and the entire world are forgiven" (Babylonian Talmud, *Yoma* 86a). We start with ourselves. It's the only place to start. And we look at our lives, where we went astray, what went wrong. Then we take a deep breath, gather what little strength is left, and go about fixing what's broken. And the act of repair gives us release from suffering and renewed strength. It's not an easy task. It's hard work. But the results will surprise you. We begin to feel alive once again, actually sensing the source of life coursing through our veins. We begin to heal as we take responsibility for self. And as we heal, the fragments of our shattered lives are made whole once again. We will never forget our past. It will serve us as a reminder of the place of suffering where our codependence can lead us. As we continue to heal, a loving God continues to forgive.

Listen to the words of one codependent person and what she did: "Even after my husband stopped drinking, I still felt guilty. I kept asking myself why I couldn't have prevented him from starting, afraid that at any time, he might start again. I wanted to do anything to save our marriage. When I finally entered recovery, someone suggested that I try the *mikvah* [ritual bath]. I go every month. When I sink into the waters and repeat the words of blessing, I feel truly cleansed, and guilt-free."

Equals. Sacred partners. Friends. All of us have a desire to maintain the special relationships we have made. In human relationships, sometimes the shattered pieces cannot be pieced back together. Sad but true. Admitting this is a difficult task. But in the admission comes liberation from suffering. By admitting you are "powerless over others," that you can't control the one you love, you can become more powerful in your own life. Quite a contradiction, but it works. Try it. See how you now feel.

A burden, taught the hasidic Rabbi Simcha Bunam, is usually carried with ease after one has become accustomed to it. When God observed that the Israelites had grown accustomed to being slaves, it was then that God decided that it was time for liberation. As they were *comfortable in their discomfort,* so are we as codependent people. It is time for your liberation.

Sometimes, other forces in our lives are so overwhelming that it takes time for us to get at the core of our codependence. This is how one codependent child of Holocaust survivors put it: "Growing up as a '2G' [second generation, child of Holocaust survivors], I always felt guilty about things. It was hard to get away from it. It seemed natural to feel that way." You have recognized that now is the time to get free of your guilt; that's why you are reading this book. You have the strength to stop suffering. Now go and do something about it.

A young man once was asked by the Gerer rebbe if he had learned Torah. "Just a little," came the reply. "That's all one ever learns of Torah," was the rebbe's response.

While the First Step is indispensable to growth, it is only the *first* step to self-care. There is much to do beyond it. Some people even say that the First Step is the only one that can actually be worked through totally. Each time, we begin again, thanking God that we are able to do so.

A LITTLE TORAH FOR THE SOUL
If you have commenced a mitzvah, continue until you have finished doing it.

Tanhuma, Ekev 6

INSIGHT FROM OUR TRADITION
Rabbi Hanina bar Idi asked, "Why are the words of Torah likened unto water?" (Isaiah 55:1). The answer: Just as water forsakes a high place and travels to a low one, so do the words of Torah find a resting place only in a person of humble spirit.

Babylonian Talmud, *Ta'anit* 7a

SOMETHING TO THINK ABOUT

The way of goodness is at the outset a thicket of thorns, but after a little distance it emerges into an open clearing. The way of evil is at first a plain, but eventually runs into a mess of thorns.

Sifre on Deuteronomy 11:6

MOVING FROM CODEPENDENCE TO COVENANT

Purify my thoughts and free me from unworthy aims.
May none of my troubles make me a stranger to You
and keep me from serving You.
Lighten the weight of other burdens that keep
me from bearing Yours, the *mitzvot* that give
me life.
So, with all my heart shall I turn to You in full
repentance.
My body and heart may fail but God is forever, the
Rock of my heart and my life's destination.

Bachya ibn Pakuda

A PRAYER FROM THE DEPTHS OF OUR HEARTS

May it be your will, Adonai, our God and God of
our ancestors, That hatred toward us shall not
arise from anyone's heart
And that hatred toward anyone else shall not
arise in our heart.
That jealousy toward us shall not arise in anyone's
heart
And that jealously toward anyone shall not arise
in our heart.
May Your Torah be our companion all our living days
and may our lives be our entreaty before You.

Based on *Berachot* 4:2

Reliance

M. GRÜNBERG / ZION GATE / JERUSALEM
OPPOSITE MOUNT ZION

Step Two

CAME TO BELIEVE
THAT A POWER GREATER THAN OURSELVES
COULD RESTORE US TO SANITY

✓ Belief is a process, not an event. It may take time.

✓ We are made "in the image" of a Power who is a loving God.

✓ A restoration of balance in our lives is possible. We can get anywhere from here, if we are willing to do so, with the help of a nurturing God.

Inherent in our relationship with a loving God is the potential for healing. It can be a model for healing our relationship with ourselves and with others.

We have to remind ourselves that belief in "a power greater than ourselves," a profound faith in God, develops over time. Step Two does not say "we believe." Instead, it says, we "came to believe." Our belief is never static. It is always changing, sometimes retreating, mostly growing. As we come to believe, we are able to let go of our dependence on others, our suffering. Hear what this codependent person told me: "I never considered myself much of a religious person. I didn't care whether God was missing from my life or not. It wasn't until I entered the program that I realized that God was always there. I just didn't look hard enough."

Don't deceive yourself into thinking that if you finally move out of the house on your own, break up with her, force your child into treatment, or even if he voluntarily enters recovery from alcoholism and other addictions, that you, too, are renewed automatically. It is not that simple. You are on the road to renewal, but you must act, take control of your own life, become a partner with your Higher Power. Powerlessness is not passivity. Once we have recognized the healing power of God, we have to seek ways to bring that healing into our lives.

It took our people forty years to get through the wilderness. Forty years from slavery to freedom. An entire generation before the Israelites were free from the shackles that bound them to their slavery. Each day away from Egypt brought them closer to Sinai and to Canaan. Every windswept step brought them closer to becoming all that they could be. Freedom was only possible when they acknowledged that it was God who could lead them home. Even Moses couldn't get them all the way there.

In the desert, there were those who rejected God's willingness to help. Others simply got lost. They never found their way back. Korach led a rebellion, deluded with the sense of his own power (Numbers 16:1-17:15). He rejected God's guidance. The earth swallowed him and his companions. A simple message with dire consequences.

Most people don't fully realize that belief is a struggle, that it does not come as easily as we would hope. They often will reject it as a possibility, because they cannot find it quickly in our culture of instant gratification. Even the most well-intentioned among us may think that if you go out and commune with nature, meditate a bit, or utter a few prayers, then you should feel connected to God for more than the moment and inspired to do holy work. It doesn't happen that way. Only great prophets and mystics can relate to God that quickly and enduringly. Those of us who are just plain folk can't depend on such special revelation. Even Moses spoke to God with halting speech.

Our sages have suggested an alternative—one should first lead a good life and then ask for religious truth (*Tana d'be Eliyahu* 162). One codependent person shared her Shabbat experience with me. She said, "I wasn't much of a Sabbath observer. Then my sponsor invited us over for Shabbat. I wanted to feel God's presence, but I just couldn't. So I decided to try it on my own. Each week I would begin by lighting the candles—and nothing happened. So I decided to let it go. By that time, lighting the Sabbath candles had become a routine. I missed it when I didn't do it—so I just continued doing it. No other reason. Then one Friday evening, I stared into the candles and they seemed to burst into flame. I was engulfed in a spiritual fire! What really hit me was the sense of peace that I felt. In the calm of Shabbat, my world was beginning to make sense once again."

God is that power that can help you feel whole again. *Shalom,* that wholesome, peaceful feeling: Sanity, serenity. All those repressed good feelings and emotions that had been lost to the agony of codependence can finally be released once again. Suffering diminishes.

For this one friend, developing a relationship with God was extremely difficult. "I always thought that God was not happy with me. I never had the feeling that God was loving and caring—even though that's what I had been taught. It hit me suddenly. It was at Sukkot. One person in my *shul* [synagogue] took us through a guided meditation. I actually felt the journey of my recovery as our ancestors took each step of their journey. I was surrounded by warmth and caring. We had walked through the desert together. I then realized God loved and cared about me."

Joseph was finally reunited with his brothers, the same brothers who had put him in a pit, told their father he had been killed, and then sold him into slavery. But he no longer felt hostile. Instead, he told his brothers that it was all part of God's plan for all of them. His hurt and anger were transformed into a profound understanding of the events that had brought him and them to Egypt. He had let his will meet the will of God. And he felt whole once again.

Meet God with me in the pages of sacred text by repeating the words that have brought comfort to generations of our people. Seek God in the air we breathe, in the food that sustains us, and in the love for self that we are trying to nurture. Surrender yourself. One mother confided in me, "I guess God really had a plan for our family. I just never realized it. I am sad that I couldn't rescue my daughter from her eating disorder. I don't even remember the me I was before she threw us into crisis. Now that I am facing my own codependence and understanding her addiction better, I have developed a real dialogue with God—and I feel alive, more than ever before. I am really grateful."

Dov Baer, known as the Maggid of Mezritch because he was a hasidic teller of tales, taught that the one who walks on the straight path of righteousness feels no special pleasure in it. That person does not even know that there is a crooked path. But the one who has first walked the crooked path and later found the direct path rejoices greatly in the discovery. In the same manner, the one who makes *teshuvah,* who turns toward God, appreciates holiness more than the virtuous person who never lost his way.

What is sanity anyway in a world that seems to care little for us? We may be tempted to believe that our "insane," uncontrolled codependence is really what's normal for us, more like life should be, because we're accustomed to it. It's part of our routine, what we have come to expect. Fully realizing that our relationships are built on our suffering, we think that they are real. But are they?

Stop trying to convince yourself of this "stinkin' thinkin'." It just shows you have been there too long. If you probe your heart deeply, honestly, you'll quickly see that codependence is robbing you of self, of "wholeness." That self can be—*will be*—restored. That "wholeness" *will be* felt. That sanity will be restored. That you can depend on.

The unknown seems frightening. A sick relationship—the one you may be stuck in right now—seems better than no relationship at all. Codependence has helped to blind us to the almost unlimited potential we hold inside of ourselves, bursting to be set free. This self has gotten lost in our relationships with others. Recognize that God can help you tap that potential. That recognition will set you free. It will illuminate your path in the unknown and light your way back into the world.

As I was growing into maturity, I would stay out later each night. My parents would leave a light on and go to sleep. They supported my independence, but still wanted to guide me as I went out into the world. When I approached the house, I would look forward to that light, its subtle glow—like a beacon—shining through the darkness. When I saw it, I knew I was home.

Faith grows over time. We reach it in uneven stages. Little by little. It's the same thing with repentance. We get there step by step. Not always in the same order, nor at the same pace. But we can't get there unless we have gone wrong. Maybe we really did have to go down and endure slavery in Egypt before we could be truly free in a land of promise. So dig deeper. Deal with your feelings. It makes the trip all the more worthwhile.

It seems crazy, but you can't experience the joy of coming back unless you have gone away. According to one talmudic rabbi, Joseph ben Halafta, God has been keeping busy since the end of creation by building ladders on which people can ascend or descend. You've fallen down. Now is the time to climb back up and take care of yourself.

Adin Steinsaltz, the contemporary religious thinker and Talmud scholar, said it this way in his book, *Teshuvah*: "The very struggle to ascend gives one the feeling of being at the bottom of the ladder; but this is only a trick of the senses and the imagination, for the ascent is, in fact, well underway."[1]

Listen to the words of my friend Rabbi Lawrence Kushner. They are from his wonderful book, *God Was In This Place and I, i Did Not Know*:

> Once we realize that what we detest in another person only wants to be accepted, taken back, and loved, do we begin to diminish our capacity for evil. By embracing what was never really other, we neutralize the evil. We heal and redeem it and, in so doing, we heal ourselves and God.[2]

As you move beyond your codependence into a relationship with a power beyond all self, remember the path you have taken, what brought you to this moment. Rejoice in the self that has been restored to you. Accept it. And thank God along the way.

A LITTLE TORAH FOR THE SOUL
One should believe that one is reborn each day.

Baal Shem Tov

INSIGHT FROM OUR TRADITION
"How do you pray to God?" asked Rabbi Nachman of Bratzlav. "Is it possible to pray with words alone? Come, I will show you a new way to God. Not with words or sayings but with song. We will sing and God on high will understand."

SOMETHING TO THINK ABOUT

God is not always silent and humans are not always blind. In everyone's life, there are moments when there is a lifting of the veil at the horizon of the known, opening a sight of the Eternal.

Adapted from Abraham Joshua Heschel

MOVING FROM CODEPENDENCE TO COVENANT

You have estranged my acquaintances from me.
You made me abominable to them.
I am imprisoned and cannot leave.
My eyes look away from affliction.
I call out to you, Adonai, every day;
I stretch out my hands to you.

Psalm 88:9–10

A PRAYER FROM THE DEPTHS OF OUR HEARTS

While King David, whom Jewish tradition calls the author of the book of Psalms, previously had bemoaned the fact that he alone must rescue himself from despair, he now calls upon God to respond to his problems by providing him a solution to his dilemma. "How long must I scheme in my spirit? . . . Answer me, my God; enlighten my eyes, before I slumber into death."

Psalm 13:3-4

Conviction

Step Three

MADE A DECISION
TO TURN OUR WILL AND OUR LIVES OVER TO GOD
AS WE UNDERSTOOD GOD

- ✓ Decisions made by you are indispensable to recovery.
- ✓ Making choices for ourselves leads us to God. With God, our will becomes God's will, our life renewed.
- ✓ Our understanding of God is a God of understanding and love.

A decision. We are thinking, feeling people who seek to regain control of our lives. As we relinquish that control to God, we actually regain it. Another contradiction of recovery. In turning to God, we are renewed. This is how one friend who entered recovery described the experience: "I thought that admitting that I was codependent was the hardest thing that I would have to do in my life. Then I made a decision to turn my will over to God. That was a tough decision, too. When you think about it, I guess the admission and the decision were both parts of the same thing."

Throughout your codependence, you probably have been trying to control other people, to manipulate them. Or maybe you think you have just been living under the control of others, doing whatever is necessary to be "loved." You might even say, as some have said to me, "I am not controlling, I am only trying to help." But don't confuse control with love. The codependent relationship and the suffering has consumed much of you. You have lost your sense of self and wholeness. You may not even realize that this control battle has overshadowed all of your relationships, making them all codependent. This control "game" has become just another manifestation of your addiction. Unlike sports and card games, there are no winners here. Everyone loses.

If you are finally ready to stop this game, turn your will over to God. Become a channel through which God's spiritual energy can flow. As the saying goes, "Let go and let God." If you aren't ready to rely on God, how can you take chances in depending on other people?

Like the other steps, Step Three is part of a process. You do not decide to turn your will over to God one day and then it happens. You have to work at it. And it's hard work. If it weren't difficult, then every codependent person would already be in recovery.

Sometimes your recovery will go smoothly, just the way you want it, with each step bringing you closer to *the God of your understanding*. But, most of the time, *we* struggle with faith—*God* struggles to reach us. Expect it and you won't be disillusioned. In that inspiring Biblical moment, Jacob wrestled with a stranger throughout the night. A stranger sent by God, reaching out from God. Some see the stranger as an angel. Others see it as the stranger within. It was not until dawn was breaking that the angel asked Jacob to let him go. The stranger could not tolerate the light. Our dark side never can. But something good came from that struggle of Jacob. He was blessed and transformed, given a new name. Recovery from codependence is such a blessing, a transforming experience.

The rabbis have taught us that redemption will not come suddenly, but we can depend on it to come, gradually, just as the sun slowly rises in anticipation of the dawn of a new day (Midrash *Shoher Tov* 18). The progress is often imperceptible; then suddenly you realize that the sun is blazing. It is, in fact, a new day for you and for your world. Rabbi Larry Kushner has taught us that "Jewish spirituality is about the immediacy of God's presence everywhere. It is about patience and paying attention, about seeing, feeling, and hearing things that only a moment ago were inaccessible."

In the *midrash* to Psalms (36:10), Rabbi Yochanan tells a story about a person who was travelling at night. His lantern went out and so he lit it again. The same thing happened several times. Each time, the man would stop and light his lantern. Finally, he decided to sit on the roadside and wait for the sunlight to arrive before he would continue his journey. Without God's light to lead the way, as this step indicates, you can't continue your journey in recovery toward renewal. It's that simple. Without God, there is no light. And in God's light, teaches the psalmist, do we see light.

Our struggle with faith is mirrored in our relationships with others. Step Three teaches us that both are part of the same struggle. Consider what this person told me:

"Twenty dollars. What harm could it do to give him twenty dollars? You can't buy drugs with twenty dollars. I thought that I was just a soft touch. It took a while, but I finally realized that I was codependent too. I really love my grandson. Our relationship means the world to me. I kept saying yes even when everyone else was saying no. When I was told that he was using the money I gave him to buy drugs, I wouldn't believe it. I was in denial. So I gave him whatever he wanted. His love was that important to me. . . . The day after I stopped giving him money, he entered rehab. I had made a decision to let God handle things. I certainly couldn't."

Once you have decided to turn your will to God, you begin to find your own path to spirituality. Don't intellectualize—just let it happen. Remember that the heart's cry to God is the highest form of prayer (*Zohar* ii, 20a).

Recovery does not mean that there will be no discord in your relationships. One person told me that he thought that every time he would argue with the woman he loved, the relationship was over. This lack of logic, this fear, is part of codependence. Realize that you are not the power in the life of others. Only God is that power. Once you acknowledge this basic truth, you can start to rebuild your relationships. Mutual trust. Faith.

To move out of your codependence, live your life differently. When you are ready to be humbled, when you have had enough of a life of shame and victimization—perhaps when you have bottomed out—follow the rabbis' advice. Express your gratitude to God by saying one hundred blessings every day. That may seem like a large number—but there really is a great deal for which to be thankful. Thank God for the good and the bad. A covenant with God is powerful, but most of all, it is filled with healing.

A LITTLE TORAH FOR THE SOUL
Before you pray that words of Torah enter your very being, pray that your sins be forgiven.

Eliyahu Rabbah 13

INSIGHT FROM OUR TRADITION
The prayer of a sick person for one's own recovery avails more than the prayer of another.

Bereishit Rabbah 53

SOMETHING TO THINK ABOUT
Rabbi Judah ben Temah urged: "Be strong as a leopard, swift like an eagle, fleet as a gazelle, and brave as a lion to the will of your God who is in heaven."

Pirke Avot 5:23

MOVING FROM CODEPENDENCE TO COVENANT
Adonai upholds those who have fallen
and raises up those who are bowed down.

Psalm 145:14

A PRAYER FROM THE DEPTHS OF OUR HEARTS

Ribbono shel Olam, Guide of the Universe and Master of Prayer, open Your lips within me for I cannot speak. Send me words to help me shape Your praise, to bring peace and blessing to my days.

Too often the world has stifled all the words of blessing within me. So much has threatened to break my spirit. Help me, Adonai, for I have been so very low, and You heal the broken in spirit with joy.

In Your compassion, in Your boundless love, give me words of prayer; then accept them from me. May my words, Your words, be sweet before You as the words of King David, sweet singer of psalms. I am so often weary, empty and dry. In thirst. In hunger, I seek comfort, even joy.

Transform my sorrow, Adonai. Help me to renew my faith, my hopes, as I raise my soul toward You. Open my lips within me, Adonai, that I may speak Your praises.

Based on Nachman of Bratzlav
adapted from *Siddur Sim Shalom,*
edited by Rabbi Jules Harlow[3]

Self-scrutiny

M. Grünberg / Zion Gate / Jerusalem
Opposite Mount Zion

Step Four

MADE A SEARCHING
AND FEARLESS
INVENTORY
OF OURSELVES

- ✓ Our codependence prevents us from seeing and being our true selves.
- ✓ Taking a fearless look at ourselves is difficult. It also can be liberating.
- ✓ So dig deeply and keep digging, but be sure to inventory *all* of you, not just the part that troubles you.
- ✓ Focus on you, not others. Look but don't judge—you or anyone else.

Without knowledge of self, there can be no honest relationship with God—or anyone else. Don't be afraid to look. You can change what you see.

Cheshbon hanefesh, an accounting of the soul, is a very Jewish concept. Life review. This is the way Judaism views the Step Four "inventory." In Jewish tradition, the entire month of *Elul,* a full month prior to *Rosh Hashanah,* is devoted to piercing moral self-scrutiny. Daily, in late summer, the penitential prayers of *selichot* get us ready for what we have to do, coaxing us, encouraging us, nurturing us, providing us with the support we need.

The Jewish calendar frequently gives us an opportunity to take a good, hard look at ourselves, wherever life has taken us. In the process of self-reflection, we are given an opportunity to draw closer to God. One friend confided in me: "It wasn't until I entered recovery that I fully understood what the High Holy Days were all about. For the first time on Yom Kippur, I truly felt like I was standing before God, chastened and renewed."

In their wisdom, the rabbis knew that to discover our true selves and build anew may take a long time. It takes more than a superficial review of recent endeavors. Look at Isaac. He had to dig the exact same wells in Gerar as had Abraham. As he dug into the soil, he also dug deeply into himself. He even gave the wells the same names as had his father. It was Isaac's own "family of origin" work. He had to journey back to his roots—before he could face his own struggle with faith. Yet he regained his strength in the saving waters of those wells.

Even a month of introspection is insufficient. So much baggage from our life travels. It is a continual process. Therefore the taking of a moral inventory should be an ongoing part of our *teshuvah,* our turning back to God. Adin Steinsaltz, Orthodox thinker and talmudic scholar, writes in his *The Strife of the Spirit* that the keystone of *teshuvah* "essentially represents a lifelong journey back to unflagging soul-searching. For it is a spiritual disquiet, much more than a guilty feeling, that makes us feel the urge to take a look back. Indeed, we feel we are no longer the right person in the right place, we feel we are becoming outsiders in a world whose scheme of things escapes us."

During the journey of the Israelites in the *midbar,* in the desert, a census was often taken. Readers of the Bible struggle to understand why God wanted the people counted so often. God instructed Moses to take an *accounting* of the people. He was not merely to count them. Rather, Moses was told to encourage them to take stock of themselves, where they had come from and most of all, where they were going. The good and the bad.

As Rabbi Lawrence Hoffman, the noted contemporary teacher and liturgist, who helped inspire the Jewish Lights Twelve Step Series writes:

> The *midbar* [desert] thus calls not so much for strength as for stamina, the stamina we need as day by day, our troubles never go away. The miracles of the *midbar* are miracles of every day: Just getting up, going through the day, going back to sleep and getting up again. To survive the *midbar,* we are allowed to count, to "number" our assets, to know in advance where our inner strength lies and what within us is on the verge of shutting down, and finally, to be reassured that we will make it, even if our personal *midbar* lasts the proverbial 40 years.

The taking of a moral inventory is one of the more onerous tasks of Twelve Step recovery. This is where many people get stuck. They go back to the earlier steps or try to skip around Step Four, hoping that another time through the other steps will help give them the strength they need to look deeply inside of themselves. We're all reluctant to look inside. We are afraid of what we will find—and so we avoid doing it. A familiar suffering may be comfortable. Maybe we focus on others so that we won't have to look inside ourselves. But without self-examination, spiritual renewal is incomplete.

For codependent persons, Step Four presents additional obstacles. As part of our own moral inventory, we have to learn not to blame ourselves for our codependent relationships. We have to stop blaming anyone. We blame others in order to avoid taking responsibility for our lives and our acts. The negative energy produced in that kind of activity is self-destructive. It is a cancer of the soul. The Fourth Step helps us to heal ourselves. Through it, as we see more of who we really are, there is more of us to love. One person told me, "I was afraid to look because of what I might find. So my rabbi helped me. We studied together and as we looked at the relationships of our Biblical mothers and fathers, I saw myself. I never saw sacred text that way before. We still study regularly, but now I'm able to do the moral inventory on my own."

Some people choose to do their inventory in the morning—often as part of morning prayers. Since Jewish tradition considers us renewed each day, the inventory helps us to look ahead. With fresh insight in hand, we get a running start into the day as it is about to unfold in front of us. *Cheshbon Hanefesh* affords us the opportunity to shape the raw material that God has just given back to us with the dawn of a new day.

Others choose to do their inventory at night, as part of a review of the day. In the still of the night, we are able to focus our thoughts as the day's experience is still painfully fresh in our minds. Even in the darkness of night, Divine light—manifest by our covenant with God—lets us see our inner selves more clearly.

Still others have recounted a different method to me. They find isolated moments during the day for mini-reviews. It helps them take their recovery one step at a time. For them, this approach makes the task a little easier. As one teacher of Judaism told me, "This too is a *madrega* [step]."

Regardless of which approach you choose, remember that there is no right way to do it. Just take pen in hand and start writing. Begin with reflective questions that do not frighten you away. Here are some starters: "I would like to be different in the following ways . . ." or "I wish I could change my world in the following ways. . . ." Remember, this really is an inventory. You have to know what it is that you have stored up and what you have gotten rid of. When you actually write it down, you will have a basis for comparison the next time. Pay attention to what was there during the last inventory and what you want to take off the shelf prior to the next one. Remember what you like about yourself, too.

This moral inventory helps ready us to humbly stand before God in the nakedness of self. For many, taking a frank look at ourselves is a unique experience. We have been hiding from ourselves for so long that we no longer know who we really are. We don't even know where to begin the process of looking, fearful of what may be revealed to us in the openness of a dialogue with self. Perhaps we may even have deluded ourselves all these years into thinking that if we didn't see ourselves, then maybe others didn't really see us either. Martin Buber, the great twentieth-century philosopher, said, "You cannot find redemption until you see the flaws in your own soul. . . . Whoever shuts out the realization of his flaws is shutting out redemption. We can be redeemed only to the extent to which we see ourselves." Facing who we really are and what we have become is the most difficult task of recovery and spiritual renewal. But it is also a turning point. It puts us in the direction we are going: Home to ourselves and a loving God.

Whenever you go on a journey, you have to prepare yourself. Moses took off his shoes before he neared the burning bush. He knew he was on holy ground. For our soul-searching, this taking of a moral inventory, we need only begin the task. But to help frame our thoughts and shape our mood, the rabbis introduced the notion of *kavannah*. More than a simple inclination to pray as the Hebrew might suggest, *kavannot* are actually verses of sacred text. When sung repetitively, generally associated with a specific melody, a *nigun,* they can help prepare us for the holy work of *cheshbon hanefesh*.

Introduce the notion of *kavannah* in your recovery to help guide your return. Here's one to get you started. It speaks to me about what *cheshbon hanefesh* means. The Hebrew text has a cadence of its own. Attend to it. It can set you free.

> *K'chu emachem, emachem devarim. Shuvu veshuvu el Hashem.*
> Take with you words [of Torah] and return to God.
> Hosea 25:2

A LITTLE TORAH FOR THE SOUL

Every single day a voice goes out from Sinai, because the giving of Torah at Sinai is forever. Like a tallis which shelters your body from the cold, it wraps your soul with its words of Torah.

INSIGHT FROM OUR TRADITION

Blessing is to be found only in a thing hidden from the eye.

Babylonian Talmud, *Ta'anit* 8b

SOMETHING TO THINK ABOUT

Who may ascend the mountain of Adonai?
Who may stand in your holy place?
The one who has clean hands and a pure heart. . . .

Psalm 24:3–4

MOVING FROM CODEPENDENCE TO COVENANT

I am weak before the wind; before the sun
    I faint, I lose my strength;
I am utterly vanquished by a star;
    I go to my knees, at length
Before the song of a bird; before
    The breath of spring or fall
I am lost; before these miracles
    I am nothing at all.

A.M. Klein,
Hath Not a Jew[4]

A PRAYER FROM THE DEPTHS OF OUR HEARTS

Provide us with the insight to our sphere and guide us as we seek to set aside the false values and vanities that creep up to steal the true richness from our lives.

From *Vetaher Lebenu,*
by the members of Congregation Beth El
of the Sudbury River Valley[5]

35

Disclosure

M. GRÜNBERG / ZION GATE / JERUSALEM
/ OPPOSITE MOUNT ZION

Step Five

ADMITTED TO GOD,
TO OURSELVES,
AND TO ANOTHER HUMAN BEING
THE EXACT NATURE OF OUR WRONGS

✓ With admitting comes cleansing and healing. When
we make our admission to God, we feel restored
almost immediately. A sense of release washes over
us and we are strengthened to do the rest of the Step.

✓ Each time we admit to ourselves a particular wrong,
we are unburdening our soul. We can actually feel
the weight of our wrongs being lifted from us. We are
declaring our readiness to face the world.

✓ Sharing with another person further relieves us of our
burden and prepares us to make changes. Start with
just one person. That's all it takes, for now.

✓ The admission process helps us determine the exact
nature of our wrongs—and of our rights. Be specific.
Don't make generalizations that cover up the real issues.
And, remember that even at our worst, our wrongs do
not consume *all* of our self. See the good also.

This Step really has three
phases—God, self, and another. Some codependent
people are able to move smoothly from one phase to
the next. Others get hung up and spend a lot of time
on one part before they are able to move beyond it.

That's OK. Admitting to God, ourselves, or anyone else that we have indeed been wrong is especially difficult when we have finally come to realize that we are not responsible for someone else's addiction or behavior.

Listen to the words of one codependent person who wants to share:

> Passover was always a time of great hope and optimism for me. The year that our awareness of our daughter's addiction became a part of our lives I thought that Passover would bring the sense of hope that had eluded me through the preceding months. It was quite the opposite. I didn't have the strength to prepare for the seder.
>
> When I was able to do Step Five and "admitted" to my rabbi, he was able to give me the perspective I needed. "You must experience the pain of slavery to fully appreciate the exhilaration of freedom," he said.
>
> His words gave me the strength to host the seder that Passover. And we will never forget his wisdom. We have participated in many *sedarim* since that time; they have new meaning for us now and connect us with renewed optimism. I realized that we are all still very much in recovery.

Do Step Five only when you are ready. Take it slowly. Begin by opening a dialogue with God. Pray. Think. Ponder. Reflect. Be comfortable in that relationship. The rabbis offer us these words of advice: "Before you pray, pray that you might pray properly." It takes some time to make the transition from the commonplace to a prayerful conversation with God. Psalms may be helpful. Or even silence. Then say what it is that you have to say. This is a time when you can stop pretending to be someone else, when you don't have to worry about what God will think of you. God already knows who you are and what you've done. The admission is for *your* sake, not God's.

Be honest. Get rid of everything that burdens you. Codependence hurts. Psychic suffering is real. This is how Rabbi Joseph B. Soloveitchik, known in Orthodox circles as "the Rav," put it: "When a Jew comes to the synagogue . . . and says, 'I have sinned, I have transgressed, I have acted perversely,' and he is racked by suffering as he says this and this anguish is due to a sense of spiritual emptiness and disaster which [is] related to acts of sin . . . the Almighty accepts such suffering. . . . [This person's] sins are considered atoned for and he can now 're-purchase' himself and make a new start in life."

A Yiddish proverb offers this advice: "God gave burdens, also shoulders." But the burdens have overwhelmed us. They weigh us down—like the straw the Israelite slaves in Egypt had to carry. Get rid of it all—the shame, the fear, the guilt, the secrets, the obsessions, the compulsions: Anything and everything that is excess baggage from a lifetime of codependence.

When we are ready to begin formal prayer in the synagogue, there is a traditional call to worship. It calls us to the task, to direct our attention to prayer. Synagogue schmoozing begins to subside. The reader chants *"Barechu et Adonai hamevorach"* which is translated as "Praise Adonai the [only] one to be praised." More loosely translated, it might read, "Are you ready to pray?"

The individual in prayer responds according to an ancient formula and, during this response, bends the knee and bows the head. It's that unique choreography which brings our full body into prayer. While the response comprises three distinct motions, after a while they flow into one, preceded by hearing the call, followed by voicing the prayer. For those in recovery, I like to compare this to the Fifth Step, for in that one moment are brought together the individual elements of Step Five, ending with talking to God.

Samson Raphael Hirsch, perhaps the most influential Orthodox Jewish thinker in the nineteenth century, considered the process of admission of wrongs this way:

> If you have recognized that you have sinned, then step into the presence of God and say: "O God, I have erred and sinned, I have been disobedient before You, I have done such and such." Feel in yourself how every sin that you have committed, however small, even in the mind and heart, immediately brings with it a curse, namely that it makes you less capable of doing good, and further inclined to sin; and when you have recognized this, then you can lay the future of your inner and outer life in the just and forgiving hand of God. And as you see yourself in spirit, so confess in word.

Some wonder why we begin the admission with God. Maimonides believed that when any person does *teshuvah* and repents, that person must confess before the Almighty. By beginning with God, it seems to make it easier for us when the time comes to admit the exact nature of our wrongs to ourselves. The only way to really know is to try.

While some might call this step magical, there's really no magic in the step. The magic is, instead, in ourselves. We have the capacity to be transformed. If you want to get ready for something new, you have to prepare. As one sponsor told me, "Trust God, trust me, then go plant some flowers."

Clean the slate. When we ready ourselves for *Rosh Hashanah* and *Yom Kippur,* everything gets cleaned and polished. Even the Torah covers are changed in the synagogue, so that, "Though our sins be as scarlet, they are now white as snow." The same holds true for Pesach—only a little more than a week long—yet we spend weeks cleaning, scouring, and cleaning some more, just to ready ourselves to experience slavery and renewal. All to get rid of the dirt, the *chametz* (the unleavened bread) in our lives.

So after you have admitted your wrongs to God, face yourself. Stand in front of a mirror, look down into a body of water—even a swimming pool. Whatever will help you focus on yourself. Speak softly. You don't have to scream—but if it helps that's OK, too. Repeat your admission over and over until you are able to really *hear* what it is that you are saying to yourself. Unlock the door of denial to your emotions. Feel with your heart the words as you say them. Take hold of these words that label your wrongdoing. Own them. Admit them, for they are yours.

But don't let them control you. Release them—along with the anger that you bear from keeping those wrongs inside you all this time. That anger, after all, is nothing more than the expression of the pain we feel from our fear of being alone, of being unloved. We know we have wronged others and we fear that they have turned from us. But our admission of wrongdoing reunites us with others, with God, and with ourselves.

Cleansed, you can now take your admission with you to someone else—just as you would introduce a new friend to one of long standing. Go ahead. Share it. Unburden yourself. Look at your wrongs through the eyes of another. It's hard. It's painful. It hurts, but it also heals and relieves your suffering.

The longer you are in recovery, the longer Step Five takes. Each time it gets better, you feel cleaner. There are layers which get peeled away each time you work this Step. It's like an old maple tree which has built up its bark to protect its trunk—yet in the spring it allows the sweet sap to flow. Savor the sweetness of your recovery. Savor the "rights" you have identified along with the "wrongs."

In your codependence, you feel beaten. In this healing dialogue with God, self, and another, you are able to reclaim the true you. As you make your way through this process of admission and through it get rid of the anger and guilt that seems to be depleting your inner strength, remember these words of hope: "The human soul is a tiny lamp kindled from the Divine torch; it is the vital spark of heavenly flame" (Babylonian Talmud, *Berachot* 10a).

A LITTLE TORAH FOR THE SOUL

Because of God, my heart exults,
Because of God, my self-respect has been restored.

From the *Haftarah, Rosh Hashanah*, First Day
1 Samuel 2:1

INSIGHT FROM OUR TRADITION

Levi Yitzchak of Berditchev was ready to conclude the Yom Kippur *Neilah* [closing] service. The *shammos* [synagogue superintendent or beadle] stood ready to sound the shofar but waited. Growing impatient, Levi Yitzchak whispered, "Why the delay?" Came the beadle's reply: "A stranger is seated near the door of the synagogue. He never learned to pray. I overheard him say to God 'Ruler of the Universe, You understand the true meaning of prayers and You know those that are the most acceptable. Since I only know the letters of the aleph-bet, I shall repeat them and You can compose from them the prayers I should recite this sacred day as part of my confession.' The Almighty is preoccupied with composing the man's prayers. Therefore, we must wait."

SOMETHING TO THINK ABOUT

If given the choice, I would prefer never to die. For in the world to come, there is no *Yom Kippur.* Of what value is life without *teshuvah?*

Rabbi Shmelke of Nikolsberg

STEP FIVE

MOVING FROM CODEPENDENCE TO COVENANT
May our petitions rise out of the night,
Our cries enter out of the dawn,
And let our joyous song appear out of the dusk.

May our voices rise out of the night,
Our vindication enter out of the dawn,
And let our redemption appear out of the dusk.

May our affliction rise out of the night,
Our pardon enter out of the dawn,
And let our cries appear out of the dusk.

O may our refuge rise out of the night,
And enter for Your sake out of the dawn,
And let our atonement appear out of the dusk.

From the piyyut "Ya'aleh," in *On Wings of Awe*
edited by Rabbi Richard Levy[6]

A PRAYER FROM THE DEPTHS OF OUR HEARTS
Your hands made me and fashioned me.
Give me understanding that I may learn your
  instruction.

Psalm 119:73

Being Prepared

Step Six

WERE ENTIRELY READY
TO HAVE GOD
REMOVE
ALL THESE DEFECTS OF CHARACTER

✓ It takes time to ready ourselves for anything. Through the first five steps, we have made ourselves fully ready, body and soul.

✓ We can reclaim our true selves with God's help, now that we are ready to rely on God.

✓ Defects in character *can* be removed, but it is up to us to keep them out.

✓ We are prepared and are ready to help a loving God heal us.

We have acknowledged our codependence and are ready to get out of this jam. Not so fast! Recovery demands readiness—and a holy dialogue. But we are afraid to move any further on our own. Still we are somewhat fearful of placing our lives in God's care. Rabbi Nachman of Bratzlav said it this way: "When fear overcomes you, subdue it by drawing yourself to God."

Codependence and addiction, like slavery, become embedded in the soul. Early members of A.A. called alcoholism "soul-sickness." When we are ready for the potential relief that spiritual renewal can offer us—at the beginning of recovery or many years into the process—we look toward God for help.

What is it that we really want God to do? What is it that we want to rid ourselves of? What is it that we want to let go of? These questions require some thought. An extensive list quickly comes to mind. After all, you have been living with the suffering of codependence for a long time. You know exactly what you can live without. But do you really? What part of you is *really* defective or is it just your relationship with others that is defective? Recognizing the difference—and the connections—is part of recovery.

We are on the road to *teshuvah* (repentance and spiritual renewal). It takes a long time to get there. As a matter of fact, we may never really get there. But we have to be ready. Each moment, each little turn we make holds unlimited potential for redemption. Each step moves us forward in our recovery but is spiritually renewing on its own. The rabbis put it this way: "One can gain a portion in the world to come in a single moment." Real *teshuvah,* one might say, is thus really a direction, not a destination.

Let go of false hopes—that's addiction—and replace them with real dreams—that's renewal. It's part of our codependence, to try to control the world around us. When we feel we can't control everything, we think we can't manage anything. We simply careen out of control and lose hold of our lives. Yet, real dreams are only possible when we are willing to allow ourselves to become part of the spiritual flow of the universe, to permit God's holiness to flow through us into the world. It is hard to let go—even harder to "let God," as the saying goes. For codependent persons, the anxiety of all separation is enhanced, even separation from unwanted thoughts and feelings. We depend on these things for structure, and the possibility of God taking them away is really hard for us to tolerate even though we want it to happen.

When you are ready to go to God, be prepared. Be in a state of spiritual readiness. Use your instincts. Under the sheltering wings of *shechinah* (God's presence), you can feel safe again.

It is still awkward for some to accept the reality that, in this relationship with God, one loses one's self. But the *chasidim* teach that in losing ourselves to God, we are able to find ourselves once again.

This is what one codependent friend related to me:

> Letting go was like sending my child out into the desert. Would she wander for forty years? Would she ever return? Would recovery of her health mean that we had to live in permanent exile from each other? I knew that it was my codependence that was holding her back, but it was the exile that I feared the most, the thought of never again being close. When I realized I had to accept the exile to give my daughter her only chance, I could let go.

It is hard for codependent parents and codependent children to let go, because often children depend on parents and parents on children for the stability we all desperately seek. And so too in all relationships.

While the rabbis of the Talmud acknowledged the necessity of God's guidance in our lives, they didn't let us off the hook so easily. These wise sages also recognized our place in the process of our own renewal when they wrote, "A place has been left for me to labor in it" (Babylonian Talmud, *Hullin* 7a). And there is indeed much work to be done. As Rabbi Harold Kushner, Conservative rabbi and author of *When Bad Things Happen to Good People,* wrote, "We cannot ask God in prayer to do something which is within our power, so as to spare us the chore of doing it."[7]

"I felt betrayed," one friend told me. "During my daughter's weigh-ins, she would put pebbles in her pockets just when I thought that my daughter was finally on the road to recovery from her eating disorder. They became stones in my soul."

Our initial responses to other's addictions really hinder their recovery because it comes from our codependence. Instead of helping, those responses "enable" the other. They build a wall of denial and bring us down, fostering our codependence. We feel like failures. But we can't just react the way we feel in our heart. Our first response, either to control or to comply, is not helpful. Many of the traditional values we learned are not really relevant.

In recovery, we have to learn a new vocabulary of healing and truly helping. As part of our codependence, words like "cheating" and "lying" mean different things; they seem to derive from a different language altogether. Concepts and instincts learned since childhood have to be rechanneled. We have to learn to "love" differently. We have to suspend our judgment; the traditional value system just doesn't quite work.

"Don't you trust me?" the addict pleads with us. "I love you and therefore will not help you destroy yourself," comes our response. Initially, this kind of response does not "feel" like love should feel. In fact, it may feel like you are withdrawing the last tie to the addicted person. Yet, this kind of loving response may be the only kind you can give to the addict you truly do love. It helps you to set boundaries in your relationships with others. This kind of loving response is indeed a gift of life—for the codependent you and for the addicted her, for the enabling you and the compulsive him. These feelings are part of our codependence. But now you can transform them with God's guidance. Just as we must provide parameters in which to live, God has also provided boundaries, *mitzvot* (holy instructions) within which to live and make our lives holy once again.

It is what the program calls a "defect in character" that constitutes our codependence, perhaps better understood as a flaw, something that prevents us from being whole, prevents our lives from being holy. In Step Six, we actually ask God to help us repair those damaged aspects of self by transforming them. God can remove these flaws; we can help.

One friend explained the feeling to me this way: "I stood there ready, waiting for God to heal me." But we both knew that she was not just waiting. In this statement, she had expressed to me the way she had taken hold of her own recovery. She knew where to turn—do you?

A LITTLE TORAH FOR THE SOUL

The one who confesses and abandons [sin] shall obtain mercy.

Proverbs 28:13

INSIGHT FROM OUR TRADITION

Meditation before God brings forth the holy spark that is in each individual Jew. It lights up the heart and thereby deprives you of all desire for evil.

Rabbi Nachman of Bratzlav

SOMETHING TO THINK ABOUT

Is that not the childhood problem—and therefore the great human problem: To learn that it is good for you when other people love other people besides you? That I have a stake in their love. That I get more when others give it to others. That if I hoard it, I lose it. That if I give it away, I get it back.

Rabbi Lawrence Kushner,
in *Honey from the Rock*[8]

MOVING FROM CODEPENDENCE TO COVENANT

Trust in God's mercies and God's kindness will encompass you. Fear God's punishments and God's strict judgments will surround you. Wherever your mind abides, you will find yourself cleaving to it. Serve Adonai in love and in complete trust and you will receive God's mercy.

Baal Shem Tov

A PRAYER FROM THE DEPTHS OF OUR HEARTS

Since I find delight in Your instruction, I petition You to guide me so that I may steadily walk in the path of righteousness.

The Apter Rav

Trust

Step Seven

HUMBLY
ASKED GOD
TO REMOVE OUR SHORTCOMINGS

✓ Coming to God is itself an act of humility, one that acknowledges the limitations of our own strength.

✓ We can't do it alone. We *ask* God, but do not make demands. We trust God to help us.

✓ Our shortcomings are repeated errors that have become routine, habits that are part of our codependence. But they are not permanent. We *can* be free of them.

With God, we can harness the spiritual energy required to recover. We may have tried, but we can't recover alone. There's nothing wrong with admitting that. Rather, there is everything right with admitting it. As a matter of fact, once you admit it to yourself, acknowledge it, believe it. You can move forward, beyond it. Own that feeling. Make it yours. In so doing, our need for a relationship with a sick other gives way to a relationship with a loving, nurturing God.

As part of understanding our own codependence, we have learned that we are not all that we once deceived ourselves into thinking we were. We are humbled. We thought that we were better than others, a suffering martyr or someone who could control another. But we weren't. It was an artificial sense of self, not our real self. It was someone who we weren't—couldn't, shouldn't have ever been. Our life was not as we pretended and told everyone that it was. The *Yom Kippur* liturgy puts it this way: "What are we? What is our life?" Now, humbled, no longer prideful, in recovery, we are much more than we ever were before. And, we are with God.

We are codependent people yearning to be healed. Yet, we are still afraid: What if we enter a relationship with God and it doesn't work either? If we ask God to remove our shortcomings—and God agrees to work them out with us—then what will be left? In recovery, we come to understand that we will be left with our true self, all that is really us.

Even so, we cannot control anyone and anything around us. Relinquishing that codependent myth of obligation and control and giving it up to God is not merely an act of humility or submission. It is an act of the spirit, a process of opening up and allowing God to influence our lives.

Some people are not comfortable with this whole notion of God taking control of our lives; they think that it is an acknowledgment of failure, that somehow they were not good enough or strong enough to make it on their own. They really miss the point. Because we are essentially good people, God doesn't give up on us. Instead, we are partners, colleagues, reliable friends. When we begin to trust in God, we can learn to trust ourselves and others once again.

One friend told me that Step Seven was the most difficult step for her. When she was in a relationship—one that she perceived to be loving—whenever she and her lover argued or fought, she thought that the relationship was over, finished, destroyed. Before her recovery from codependence, she thought that good relationships were supposed to be totally free from arguments. No disagreements. No independence. A relationship in which one cares for and depends on the other. But that's a Hollywood myth. Her parents had argued frequently. They verbally abused one another with words of "loving" guilt, so she wanted nothing to do with that kind of sick relationship. But she was apprehensive nonetheless. She was downright scared. If she turned to God and there were disagreements, then *that* relationship could be doomed also. Being caught in the middle paralyzed her. After her divorce, she sought recovery. Now she is able to see where she had gotten lost. She still struggles with this Step, but she knows how important it is. After all, it was God who helped her to understand and shed this shortcoming.

How does it all work? Do you just go to God and poof! the shortcomings are gone? If only it were that easy. In recognizing that your weaknesses are there, you have already begun the process of removing them. God helps by giving you the strength to see your way through it.

The process in this Step is best captured for some in this phrase from the Hallel psalms: "*Ana Adonai, hoshiah nah. Ana Adonai, hatzlicha nah.*" "I beg You, God. Save me. Rescue me." Mull these words over. I often do. Let their rhythm become a part of your everyday *kavannah* meditation before prayer, before you consciously do this Step.

Rabbi Lawrence Hoffman, contemporary writer and liturgist, described our unique relationship with God in this Step wonderfully when he wrote:

> In the Tefillah, [the central prayer for Jewish worship] the second to last blessing is called "Thanksgiving," *Modim,* the prayer *par excellence* where Jews offer thanks to God. But what do we thank God for? "We give thanks for Your miracles that are with us day by day, for Your wonders and goodness of every moment: Morning, noon, and night."

> These then are the miracles that matter, the miracles of the *midbar,* [the desert] the day-by-day getting through our own personal dry spells, when we get up each morning to a world apparently without suste-nance, and lie down each night feeling coldly alone, surrounded only by darkness that does not dissipate.

> Each of us enters our own *midbar* once in a while; infrequently if we are lucky, but at least once, and maybe more often, and maybe also for a long time. Deserts seem then to stretch endlessly ahead; promis-ing oases turn out to be mirages. Our stamina flags. But the story of our ancestors reminds us that we can get through. The Promised Land of milk and honey lies somewhere in the distance. And, in the meantime, we number the things within us that God has supplied for just such times as this, the day-by-day miracles that sustain us, and for which we give thanks.

What a message of hope! What a message for all those in recovery from codependence!

But it's not so simple for all of us. As one woman told me:

> As a Jewish. woman, as a mother, I had hoped to shield the people I love from pain. My daughter's addiction threw our entire family into a reexamination of ourselves and our relationships. We are different people now, all the much stronger, much more independent. We would never go back to being the people we were before this began. One of the most difficult steps I took was to forgive myself for most of the things I did that were part of an unhealthy codependent family pattern that harmed my child. I also can now see how I was liberated by our family's recovery. But I must admit that there will be a little piece of me that will always be saddened because my child redeemed me—instead of the other way around.

Redemption. That's what recovery is really all about. Once you have recognized that the removal of your shortcomings is part of the redemptive process, then you are ready to go on to the next step. Don't worry. You'll be back working this one again. We all do.

A LITTLE TORAH FOR THE SOUL
Baruch Adonai yom yom. God is to be blessed every day. Every day is a gift. We are challenged to put this gift to good use.

INSIGHT FROM OUR TRADITION
Fill yourself with compassion and *Adonai* will be filled with compassion toward you.

Bereishit Rabbah 33.3

SOMETHING TO THINK ABOUT

The one who covers his wanton acts will not succeed.

Proverbs 28:13

MOVING FROM CODEPENDENCE TO COVENANT

The Medziboner rebbe taught: "A traveler came to a town where everyone was a stranger to him and he had no one with whom to converse. Later another stranger arrived and both became friends, impelled by their mutual loneliness. They agreed to have no secrets from one another. The psalmist says (119:19), I am a stranger in the earth of evildoers and You, *Adonai,* are likewise unwelcome. Let us become friends and have no secrets from one another."

A PRAYER FROM THE DEPTHS OF OUR HEARTS

Adonai, I have done You intentional wrongs; I have done You willful wrongs; I have even rebelled against You. I have done this and this particular act. Now I feel ashamed and full of regret for my acts, and I will never repeat this thing that I have done.

From the *Al Cheyt* confessional prayer,
from the Service for the High Holy Days

Readiness

Step Eight

MADE A LIST
OF ALL PERSONS WE HAD HARMED,
AND BECAME WILLING
TO MAKE AMENDS TO THEM ALL

✓ Make a list, any kind will do, but it is important to
write it down.

✓ Start with the little hurts. Once you are strong enough,
include the more serious harm you may have done. All
of us *have* hurt others and ourselves. Acknowledge it.

✓ Be willing to take the first step toward atonement.
This is preparation for redemption.

✓ A willingness to make amends brings the circle of
recovery, and our lives, closer—to the heart and
the soul.

Wait a minute, you say.
We are the ones who were harmed! We are the ones
who were mistreated, even abused. Why should we
make a list? Whom did *we* harm?

That's the point. We see ourselves as victims—and project victimizing onto others, even beyond our
codependent other to many with whom we come into
contact. Neighbors. People with whom we work.
Employers, employees, store clerks and repair people.

It's part of the codependent filter through which we view the world. Shatter that filter. Replace it. By working this step, we can move beyond our own real or imagined victimization. Recovery and renewal gives us the strength to say out loud: "With God's help, we will be victims no more. We will also make no victims."

A person in recovery told this to me after a recent meeting: "I felt funny about making a list, but I was committed to doing whatever was asked of me. I was so desperate to recover. So I started a Step Eight diary. When I began, the lists were long, pages and pages of people I had hurt. It took writing it down for me to realize all the pain *I* had caused. As my recovery progressed, the lists got shorter. I was much more conscious about what I was doing and saying. I still make the lists. It's my own Book of Life."

I like to call this Step part of making *teshuvah* in the heart. That's where it really belongs. Step Eight demands a fundamental change in attitude, one that is more than simply logical, rational. Step Eight requires us to think very differently from the way we are used to thinking. We can't blame our codependence on our codependent other's addiction or behavior. Just take responsibility for our own actions, our own responses to the challenges of everyday living. It's all very difficult. It's painful. We suffer. But it's so healing.

One friend told me that this year she wanted to approach God on *Yom Kippur* without the heavy heart that had accompanied her in all the years of her husband's addiction and her own codependence. So this time, she asked forgiveness of her former husband. He had abused her during his drinking and she had permitted it, but she had wanted to preserve her family at all costs—including those to herself. She had really convinced herself that she could get him to stop drinking, but she had confused sex with love. So she stayed in this codependent marriage until she entered recovery. That *Yom Kippur,* for the first time, she felt able to face God honestly.

Saying "no" has always been hard for us. Because we wanted to be loved, we did anything, tolerated anything—sex, drugs, alcohol, food, physical and emotional abuse—even when we were not driven by our own needs. We did things, went places—all because we were absolutely terrified to say "no." Would it contribute to her addiction? Would it cause him to drink again? Would he hit me? Would she abuse me with guilt?

In recovery, we learn how to say "no," to set boundaries in relationships, and then perhaps walk away—if necessary—sometimes for a long time, sometimes forever. It's not without effort. It requires "detachment." At first it will seem nearly impossible. The words stick in our throats. We practice the process over and over, just to get the scenario right. But then it blows up in our faces. Yelling. Screaming. Insults. Doors slam. It takes time to realize that when we do say "no" it does not mean that we want to harm or hurt people. Yet, often, saying "no"—while the right thing to do—is indeed hurtful. It can also end a relationship. But face the facts. You may only be able to save yourself. Even if the relationship is worth saving, your active codependence can destroy it. It will not help the relationship or you and will certainly not convince the other in your life to stop drinking or using or gambling or eating compulsively or running around. But your recovery can nurture a relationship with God while it nurtures you at the same time.

So take it easy. Begin with people with whom you do not have such an intimate or complicated relationship. Leave the dishonesty behind you. Once you have gathered the courage and the strength, break out of your codependence. Say "no" even to those you love, those who may have contributed to bringing you down. Say "no" to them all—but say "yes" to recovery.

Listen to how one friend has approached it: "How could I refuse to buy my mother groceries? I would not give her money because she would spend it on liquor. I was clever. I took her to the grocery store. I saw everything that she put into her cart. But since I bought her the food, she used the money to buy booze. I was in denial. Now I am ready to make amends."

Remember when you would do anything with her—just to be with her? Well, it's over. So saying "no" starts our Step Eight process of making amends.

Some people change their names in recovery. Anonymity is not enough for them. They feel that a name change gives them new life. Jacob—after his struggle—became Israel. He was renewed by his struggle, transformed. Think about it. It is as if to say, "I am someone else, not that person who did those things." But we are those people. We *did* do those things to others and to ourselves. Making a list helps us to face that fact.

For those in recovery from codependence, working Step Eight may be the spiritual breaking point, that first real spiritual crunch that you hit. It's funny how you expect it to come when you confront your belief in God. But it hits you—like so many other things—when you least expect it: When you confront your belief in yourself.

Some codependent people choose to go to meetings for alcoholics, for people with chemical addictions. They tell me it gives them hope for their own recovery, that recovery is possible, they too can recover—from codependence. For you, recovery from codependence seems more onerous than from alcoholism or drug addiction, eating disorders or compulsive sex. You know what alcohol tastes like, what drugs look like. It's harder to identify the poison of our codependence. But it's toxic nonetheless. That's why this step is so important to work and work again. And then work it some more. Once we are able to better understand our codependence, and our role in it, we can realize that, in fact, even though we often *felt* like victims, we were the primary source of our own pain. In response to our suffering, we struck out at others, sometimes at those who seemed to hurt us least. Meaningless retaliation. Revenge. Recognizing all this does not absolve the other in your life. They still have to recover on their own. But it does free us.

Don't beat yourself up by thinking that you have harmed the world, that everyone with whom you have come into contact has been harmed. Instead, first think about the people you have touched positively and build from there. There will be those whom you have harmed. We all have harmed others, among them the ones we love the most and want least to harm. We are not perfect in our behavior. That's reality. But from now on, you can change it.

Once you have made your list, think about how you might want to make amends. Entering recovery, taking responsibility, already tops that list. Entering recovery is your first step toward making those amends. Consider various alternatives. Think about what would be important, meaningful to the person you have harmed, not what would just be comfortable for you. Don't try to do anything that you can't do, that you are not able to do, that you are not ready to do.

You aren't supposed to do anything yet. That will come in the next step. Remember: One step at a time. Just think it through. Don't "double-think," that codependent way of worrying only about what other people will think of what you do. Just consider how you might right some of the wrongs that resulted from your codependence, *including those you did to you.* Thinking through this process of atonement helps ready us for that next step and for relationships in which we don't repeat our codependent behavior.

A LITTLE TORAH FOR THE SOUL
The Baal Shem Tov, the founder of the Hasidic movement, known as the *Besht,* taught: "In every good deed, there is a littleness and a greatness. If one does Torah with little attention, it is littleness. But if one concentrates on one's deeds, there is greatness."

INSIGHT FROM OUR TRADITION

The individual cannot make oneself wicked.

Babylonian Talmud, Bava Metzia 3b

SOMETHING TO THINK ABOUT

I recognize my wantonness.
My sin is before me always.

Psalm 51:5

MOVING FROM CODEPENDENCE TO COVENANT

My heart was not haughty nor my eyes lofty;
and I did not concern myself with things too great
and too wonderful for me.
Have I not calmed and quieted my soul?

Psalm 131:1-2

A PRAYER FROM THE DEPTHS OF OUR HEARTS

Judge of all the earth
that now in judgment stands,
grant life and mercy
to a people poor, indigent.
May the prayer of the morning
take the place of sacrificial offering,
May the offering of the morning
be the sacrifice we make.

David ben Eleazar ibn Pakuda, 12th C
from the Selichot prayers
on the day before Rosh Hashanah
and the morning of Yom Kippur

Change

Step Nine

**MADE DIRECT AMENDS
TO SUCH PEOPLE WHEREVER POSSIBLE,
EXCEPT WHEN TO DO SO WOULD INJURE
THEM OR OTHERS**

✓ Do what you have to do directly. Don't place others in the middle, don't be indirect in what you say or do. Let your actions speak for your intentions.

✓ It may not always be possible to make amends. All we can do is try.

✓ Be cautious. Be caring. Be vigilant. You do not want to cause additional pain.

Making amends means that we have changed. We can't sit still. Recovery from codependence requires that we act. Such atonement has a way of healing the past.

But, it can't be said enough: It's not going to be easy. You spent a lot of years as an active codependent. Undoing the damage does not go so quickly. You may be ready to approach others, but your recovery time-clock may not be in sync with those around you. They may not be ready to hear, to listen to your apology, no matter how sincere it may be. Don't be disheartened. Don't give up. You have already come too far. Are you ready to approach yourself?

Build up your courage, the resolution of spirit to confront the past. In doing so, you will have the strength to face the future. Saying "I'm sorry" may be inadequate. Perhaps you have said it too many times before. Perhaps it will be turned against you. But that's where to begin nonetheless.

Through Step Nine, you will be able to begin to reclaim some of the healthy relationships that may have been lost to codependence. Not all of them, but some of them. Certainly that most important one—your relationship with yourself.

When you work the program, relationships will change. With this change comes a sense of panic. "What's coming next?" we ask ourselves. As painful as any one relationship may have been, you could always count on it, depend on it, know what to expect. This fear of the unknown may undermine your desire to continue in your recovery. This is the point at which it is important to lean on the steps you have already taken. Trust yourself and the process. Like the steps in Jacob's ladder, each one is critical. Each one brings you closer to the next—and to Heaven. Like Jacob, we have learned that it is not possible to complete our dream unless we have the courage to step on every rung of the ladder.

"Living with an addict had completely distorted my sense of reality and the way I cope with the outside world," a new friend told me. "My children stopped bringing friends home because they were afraid that my husband, their father, would embarrass them. I urged them to take after-school jobs so that they might return home *after* he had fallen into his customary drunken sleep. Now they are away at college, and I realize how much of their lives I have missed."

Take one relationship at a time and try to improve it. It will take time and hard work. You've probably been codependent for much of your life. You can't expect to undo everything overnight. And, an exciting prospect: With the help of this step, you can work on building new, loving, healthy relationships.

For some, relationships are an all-or-nothing experience. Often, codependent people only know extremes: Intense friendships or passing acquaintances. Middle ground in everything, including relationships, is the toughest of all. One friend told me, "I have no sense of moderation. I still don't know how to discern the middle ground." Making amends to people and starting over in relationships helps make us able to rebuild relationships without getting caught in their web; we can find that comfortable middle ground.

It's funny how our codependence seemed to help us in crises—especially with our codependent other. In those crises, we were able to shut down major emotions. We thought we were protecting ourselves and doing good for the other. And maybe we were, at first. But in doing so, we shut out the self we must also love. Now as we see what this shutdown cost us—and everyone around us—we are afraid to shut down when it is necessary.

As has been said with the other Steps as well, *teshuvah* is the essence of Step Nine. Making amends. Changing the direction of our lives. Returning to the path that God had originally intended us to follow. We literally turn from the direction we had been going and go the other way. Along the route, we go to people and ask for their forgiveness, trying to make up for the wrongs we caused, the damage we did. *Teshuvah* means that the opportunity to go back and try again is always available to us.

Step Nine teaches us not just that we are going to try to make amends. It also means that we are going to stop trying to tell people what they should think, how they should truly feel even about our atonement. That's what we were doing in our codependence. Let people feel the way they want—including the way they want to feel about us. What you say and do may not change the way they feel about you, but this act of contrition will help change the way you feel about yourself.

Whether you have a *written* list or not, you know whom you have harmed, you know it all too well. But Step Nine is not only about making amends to others; it is also about trying to reconcile, to make peace, with those who have harmed us, to take care of "unfinished business" that may be lingering for a long time, even since childhood. Simply avoiding those you love and those who love you is not part of recovery. It may initially have given you the space you needed to sort things out, but eventually—through this step—you will have to confront the feelings and the people directly. But wait until you are ready. Take the time and space you need. Work through your own feelings, unburden yourself in the fullness of Step Five before you go to others. You can't have *shalom bayit* (peace in your home) without first being at peace with yourself. Serenity. *Shelemut* (tranquility and wholeness).

Teshuvah means that you will have to forgive others. But face it, we don't always feel so forgiving. Until we have worked this Step fully, we may still feel that there are those who don't even deserve our forgiveness. We feel so deeply hurt that we just can't bring ourselves to forgive let alone ask for forgiveness. We feel cheated, robbed—often of our childhood, sometimes of our "best years."

Some people find that they can do things to help place themselves in a forgiving mood. They may reflect in their minds things they have already forgiven others. Or they may think about what others have forgiven about them and the things they have done. If others can forgive what we have done, surely we too can be forgiving. I find that prayerful music provides me with the spiritual buoyancy I need when I don't feel so forgiving. To be lifted heavenward in prayer helps frame my mood and then I'm better ready to forgive. God gives me the strength, especially in those times when I can't seem to find it on my own. When I remember that God forgives all that I have done, I am quickly moved to forgive others.

Step Nine demands that we take responsibility for our lives and what we have so far done with it. But it also provides us with the opportunity to take responsibility for its future direction as well. It's a form of spiritual maturity. Stop feeling guilty about what you have done and instead, go and do something about it. Trust the process. It can work for you if you work it for yourself. Working Step Nine will help us to feel good about our behaviors and likewise good about ourselves. It provides us with an opportunity to refashion our behaviors once we have repaired the damage they have caused. Freed somewhat of these past burdens—that's what Step Nine helps us to do—we can try out the new behaviors recovery has taught us. These new approaches to familiar situations will help us to lead holy lives, lives of wholeness.

A LITTLE TORAH FOR THE SOUL
Transgressions extinguish the light radiated by *mitzvot* but they do not extinguish the light of Torah.

Babylonian Talmud, *Sotah* 21a

INSIGHT FROM OUR TRADITION
Whoever finds nothing but faults in others is himself full of faults. That person never finds anything good to say about anyone.

Derech Eretz Rabbah I
Based on a translation by Danny Siegel in
Where Heaven and Earth Touch[9]

SOMETHING TO THINK ABOUT
Let your heart be whole with Adonai.

I Kings 8:61

CHANGE

MOVING FROM CODEPENDENCE TO COVENANT

Blessed is my Higher Power whose love and compassion has led me to this wonderful fellowship.

Blessed is the compassionate One who has given me a program that has changed my life.

Blessed is the Master of the Universe who gave me Twelve Steps to live by.

Blessed is the sovereign One to whom our praise is due.

Blessed is the Holy One who inspired those who gave us a program of recovery.

Blessed are those who came before us and showed us the way.

From the JACS Shabbat Morning Service
Used with permission

A PRAYER FROM THE DEPTHS OF OUR HEARTS

May the source of strength
Who blessed the ones before us,
Help us find the courage
To make our lives a blessing. . . .

Bless those in need of healing
With *r'fu-a sh'lei-ma,*
The renewal of body,
The renewal of spirit,
And let us say, Amen.

From *"Mi Shebeirach,"*
by Debbie Friedman and Drorah Setel, 1988[10]

Confession

Step Ten

CONTINUED
TO TAKE PERSONAL INVENTORY
AND WHEN WE WERE WRONG,
PROMPTLY ADMITTED IT

✓ Continuing means that you don't stop and you never will. The process of self-examination started in Step Four and continues in Step Ten.

✓ Recovery is a lifelong process. So is the process of self-scrutiny, of personal inventory.

✓ When you are wrong, you're wrong. Admit it. Stop blaming others. It is not possible to be right all the time; that's part of being human.

✓ Don't look for excuses. Face yourself and what you've done. And then be done with it. Don't carry the burden or the baggage.

*T*here is always more to learn about ourselves, no matter how far on the road of recovery and renewal we have travelled. And as life goes on, we are constantly changing. Whether, in fact, we are in recovery or not, we are always on the way to fully knowing ourselves. And self-knowledge will always help us reach closer to God, closer to wholeness, and closer to healthy and loving relationships.

Through Step Ten, we have a better chance of recognizing more quickly when we have gone astray. In the program, this is what might best be called "owning our power." It is knowledge of self and more. Such knowledge does not mean that we will do no wrong. We will. We are all human. There is no avoiding temptation; it is part of life.

The rabbis called the basic human drives *yetzer tov* (good inclination) and *yetzer hara* (evil inclination), but they recognized that both are necessary and indispensable for the survival of self as people with free will. Yet, they also taught that we can change our response to the *yetzer hara,* this inclination to do evil. So when we do err, working Step Ten gives us a chance to make the repair more readily. Sometimes it is just knowing when it is time to walk away and "chill out," what the program calls "detachment." We have to depend on ourselves, we have to be constantly aware of what we say and do. Others won't always tell us when we are wrong—even those we love. They may be afraid—as we once were—to speak the truth. Truth demands personal courage. Such courage comes from spiritual renewal. The prophet Zechariah sensed it when he taught, "Not by might, nor by power, but by the spirit [of God] alone shall we live with [inner] peace." This Step helps us to learn how to love ourselves once again and avoid the self-neglect which is a result of our codependence, so that we can live in peace with ourselves.

Rabbi Lawrence Kushner put it this way in his *God Was in This Place and I, i Did Not Know,* in which he teaches us some of the many messages of Jacob wrestling with the angel:

The unnamed night wrestler of Genesis 32 represents a dimension of ourselves that has been rejected and labeled as "evil other." It comes back to injure and maim us during the night. And since it is still a part of ourselves we cannot bear to acknowledge, when we sense it in someone else, we are all the more frightened and angry. And often, failing to find it in someone else, we project it onto them anyway for this deludes and comforts us into feeling that we have utterly torn it away. Hating something in someone else is easier than self-reproach.[11]

Listen to what this father told me: "I could not comprehend what the therapist meant when she told me that the only way I could help my daughter was to change myself. My daughter engaged in compulsive behaviors, but I was fine! Yet, I was wrong—I know it now. I was not fine. I felt as empty as my daughter did. She had looked for meaning in her life and got lost. I didn't even know to look. Gaining my strength made it possible for her to gain hers."

Just because this Step is number ten among twelve does not mean that you have to wait until you get to this point to get started on it. The process of self-reflection is continuous, ongoing, even while you are working and reworking the other Steps. That process never stops. And don't think that you only have to do Step Ten prior to *Yom Kippur* or before you approach God in prayer. Just make it part of your daily routine for renewal. Step Ten really should help provide us with a filter on the world and our place in it. The focus is always on self examination, not on the judging of others.

Let your codependence work for you. If you see something you don't like in another person, chances are it probably is in you, too. Change it there inside *your* soul. In codependence, the emphasis is on everyone and everything but ourselves. Recovery allows us to focus on ourselves and be healed as a result. That's why Step Four and Step Ten seem similar, but they really are not. Step Four helps us clear away the initial debris. Step Ten helps us to better understand the self once we have found it.

But don't just focus on the negative. There is much positive in our lives and in ourselves. Love it all. And love thyself. Remember, though you are nothing but dust and ashes, you are also little lower than the angels, made in the image of a loving God. Living a spiritual life in recovery is living in the balance.

There is a saying around the rooms that "Every codependent is an addict and every addict is a codependent." One codependent addict told me that when he would first enter into a relationship with someone, everything would be fine. Then something would go wrong, something very simple that needed to be worked out. But he would become emotionally paralyzed. He shut down, avoiding any kind of reconciliation. The relationship had to be perfect or not at all. Afraid of more suffering, he started drinking to nullify the pain. After all, it worked for his father. Or so he thought. But then the pain got worse. The relationship was gone, destroyed. So he quickly entered a new relationship. He yearned for an intimacy that he was unable to find. He felt that he desperately needed a relationship of any kind even though it was bound for the same conclusion. And thus the painful cycle of codependence kept turning.

For codependent people, this kind of compulsive relationship is itself addictive. Alcohol or drugs may not be involved on the part of the codependent, yet codependent people may all be on the same train as the addict; some just don't travel as far.

Self-hate is serious suffering. It forces us to run from one relationship to another, because we can just never connect to people. This is at the essence of codependence.

It crosses the generations, often the result of being an adult child of an alcoholic or other addict or seeing parents engage in compulsive behaviors. One friend told me, "I grew up not feeling very good about myself. But I really never thought that my family was very dysfunctional. I always thought that I was supposed to take care of everyone else, that I was supposed to do whatever I was told to do, whatever anyone else wanted me to do. I just carried this myth from my childhood into my adulthood, but I guess I always remained a child nonetheless."

Step Ten reminds us that recovery is a process, one that we have to continually carry on. Keep changing. It's well worth the struggle.

A LITTLE TORAH FOR THE SOUL
In my youth, when I was filled with the love of God, I thought I could convert the whole world to God, but soon I discovered that it would be quite enough to convert the people who lived in my own town. I tried for a long time, but I did not succeed. Then I realized that I was still too ambitious, and so I concentrated on the members of my family. But I couldn't change them either. Finally, I realized that I must work on myself, so that I might give true service to God. I am still working on myself.

The Rabbi of Zans

INSIGHT FROM OUR TRADITION
The greatest sinner is the one who regrets his previous goodness.

Zohar iii, 101a

SOMETHING TO THINK ABOUT
The Holy Blessed One said, "If you give me your heart and your eyes, then I know you are mine."

Jerusalem Talmud, *Berachot* 1:5

MOVING FROM CODEPENDENCE TO COVENANT
Every Jew possess some good trait, pleasing to *Adonai,* but no one of us is able to diagnose the self adequately to discover what that trait is. You may be sure that the qualities which bring you self-aggrandizement are not those which *Adonai* approves in you.

Rabbi Yehudah Aryeh Leib of Ger

A PRAYER FROM THE DEPTHS OF OUR HEARTS

Hear our voice, You, Our God,

Protect us, have mercy upon us;

Accept in mercy and with favor our prayers.

Do not cast us aside, as we grow old,

As strength has waned,

Do not desert us.

From the penitential prayers of the *Selichot* service

Worship

M. GRÜNBERG / ZION GATE / JERUSALEM
OPPOSITE MOUNT ZION

Step Eleven

**SOUGHT THROUGH PRAYER AND MEDITATION
TO IMPROVE OUR CONSCIOUS CONTACT WITH GOD
AS WE UNDERSTOOD GOD,
PRAYING ONLY FOR THE KNOWLEDGE OF GOD'S WILL
FOR US AND THE POWER TO CARRY THAT OUT**

- ✓ Prayer is a conversation with God, meditation a conversation with self. Prayer and meditation help you find out where you are going and how to get there.
- ✓ Meditate before prayer. Pray before you meditate. Both nurture the soul and the self and bring the Divine Presence into your life.
- ✓ Pray for an understanding of God's response to your prayers, for the strength to build healthy and loving relationships, not for things.
- ✓ Then act, make your prayers reflective of the life you want to lead.

In codependence, you "live for the other." Here you live for God and want to carry out God's will, not the will of the codependent other. You ask for the strength to be healthy, to recover. But it is no mystery to know God. It may be easier than you think. Rabbi Samuel Dresner, a Conservative Rabbi and well-known teacher of *teshuvah,* put it this way in his *Three Paths of God and Man*: "God's glory fills the world, it is true; but just as the radiance of the sun, reaching everywhere, can be closed off by the palm of the hand before the face, so can the glory of God be shut out by the wall of the will before the soul."[12]

In order to know "God's will," you simply have to be willing to rebuild your relationship with God just as you have begun to rebuild your relationship with self and others. We begin with prayer and meditation. The rest follows. Keep it up. Make prayer part of your recovery routine. Let it flow into your religious life. You'll soon find that there is little difference between recovery and spiritual renewal. Through Step Eleven, a spiritually religious Judaism helps shape your recovery, anchoring it and you at the same time.

Some people are not so comfortable with all of this God-talk. They don't see it as very Jewish. And so they avoid it as they avoid the many opportunities that Judaism offers us to do *teshuvah*. What a pity. In recovery, we can learn how to seek out God and be renewed. But don't think that mere ritual observance will do the trick. It seems strange advice from a rabbi. But listen hard. If religious observance is part of your attempt to be a better person, fine. But if you are doing it to please God in the same way you tried to please people as part of your codependence, forget it! Stop living that same lie. God does not reward you just because you do more *mitzvot* (the fulfillment of God's holy instructions) today than you did yesterday. That's not the way it goes. You do *mitzvot* because you want to do them. The reward is in the doing. Get to know the feeling. And be swept heavenward.

In his wonderful book, *God Was in This Place and I, i Did Not Know,* Rabbi Lawrence Kushner taught us:

> The beginning of knowing about God, in other words, is simply paying attention, being fully present where you are, or as Rashi [the medieval commentator] suggests, waking up. We realize, like Jacob, that we have been asleep. We do not see what is happening all around us. For most of us, most of the time, the lights are on but nobody's home.[13]

When the Torah relates to us the people's reaction to the revelation at Mount Sinai, it reports that the people were terrified. Nevertheless, they responded by saying, "*Naaseh venishmah*—we will do and we will hearken [to God's voice]." Through the doing comes understanding. But *lishmoah,* to hear, means more than just understanding. The people were afraid. Moses told them not to worry. God tests at first to see whether we are ready to handle an intimate, loving relationship with God, just like God did with Abraham and Sarah, Isaac and Rebeccah, Jacob, Rachel, and Leah. Through living a holy life, one filled with *mitzvot,* we ready ourselves for that relationship—we long for it.

Don't expect to experience spiritual ecstasy the first time or every time you experience the holy—or even at all. The simple routine is what makes the religious life so special. The experience of God is in the holy relationship you establish, what we call covenant. Daily life feels like Sinai because you want to be there. Even in simple routine. Really "being there" is a whole different plane of existence. It's really hard to explain, much easier to experience, as long as you are looking in the right places. Through Step Eleven, we learn that recovery is one of those right places.

Rabbi Menachem Mendl of Kotzk, one of the most insightful of the hasidic rebbes, helps us to understand. He was puzzled why God invited Moses up to the mountain in order to receive Torah and "be there," as the Torah tells us. The Kotzker rebbe advised, "Even one who strains himself to ascend onto a high mountaintop, and is indeed able to reach the summit, it is nevertheless possible that he is still not there. Even though he may be standing on the very peak itself, his head may be somewhere else." To find God and reach the holy in your life, your head has to be in the right place, seeking "the knowledge of God's will for us."

When the Israelites built the desert *mishkan,* the portable sanctuary, it was not because they believed that God might dwell in it, as a quick reading of the account might suggest. Rather, the *mishkan* helped them to direct their spiritual yearnings—"to improve [their] conscious contact with God"—and God could dwell among them. Holy places are not places where God dwells more intensely. They are "holy" because the mood we've created there allows us to perceive God's presence more readily. Step Eleven helps us clear the clutter from our heads and our hearts so that we can indeed perceive the presence of God more clearly. Thus, the importance of Sinai for our recovery is not just in what we have learned about the holy *content* of Torah, but also in the holy *context* of Torah: In the meeting of God and the individual.

What the Torah has to say to us about living a *holy* life and making our lives *whole* once again goes without saying. But the real message is much more subtle. The encounter at Sinai between God and the people, that awesome moment of silence (and serenity) is what gives real significance to Torah. That moment floods our souls. It's that moment that Step Eleven helps us recapture every time we work it, every time we set out once again to redirect our lives. It's a constant turning.

Listen in on this conversation that I had with a friend who came to talk to me as he searched for the holy: "Shabbos was the most difficult day of the week," he told me. "I felt isolated. Shabbos was the same for everyone else but me. I couldn't go to a meeting—and I needed to. I yearned for a religious place. I had not found it in the synagogue. At meetings, at least they talked about God." So we walked together, sought the holy together, teacher and student together. We talked, we laughed, we prayed. We learned from one another that prayer without direction of the heart is like a body without a soul. It is not enough to do what is right; what we do must be done with our whole being.

As we have come to understand, recovery is an act of covenant—an individual walking with God—guided and inspired by others in our community, in our fellowship. The others who have joined us in our journey are significant. Without them, we would have to go it alone—and we know that we can't. Perhaps we may have even tried it and found that we couldn't. Don't be embarrassed. There is no shame there. The myth of independence is just another one of those myths that we have to shed as we recover from our codependence and enter into a renewed and constantly renewing relationship with God.

The journey to the holy is much the same. Ultimately, we have to seek God on our own, but we benefit from the wisdom, the guidance, the past experiences of others. It's not easy finding a spiritual guide who can help us plumb the depths of our soul and help us reach heavenward as well. Jewish tradition provides us with some guidance: "If a teacher resembles an angel from God, seek Torah from that teacher" (Babylonian Talmud, *Moed Katan* 17a). Search out a teacher as you have found a sponsor with whom you can search your soul and go beyond the limits of your own experience.

Don't be afraid of what you don't know. Recovery helps you recognize that it is OK to say, "I just don't know." Imagine instead what you can potentially learn! Remember, "The Holy Blessed One wants [only] the heart" (Babylonian Talmud, *Sanhedrin* 106b). What's really great is that we don't have to go out looking for God. God is there looking for us as well. The eleventh-century Spanish poet, Bachya Ibn Pakudah, said it all when he wrote:

> I have sought your nearness,
> With all my heart have I called out to You,
> And going out to meet You,
> I found You coming toward me.

How can we know what it is that God wants us to do with our lives if we have not established a relationship with God? This then is the real goal of Step Eleven. Through working this Step, we can enter into worlds we have never explored before. In our active codependence, we may have thought we knew it all, had it all. But, as we have learned, we weren't even close. We want to live, really live. And now we are ready to do so.

And so we pray that we might begin to understand God as we begin to understand ourselves, and that we might have the power to act on that understanding. Just remember you may not be able to make everything all right, but through Step Eleven and the "knowledge of God's will for us" you can avoid making it all wrong.

"I pray," an acquaintance told me in the synagogue, "I pray that God might help me discover what to do. After every encounter with her family, my wife resorts to food. I want her to choose life for herself. It's selfish. I admit it. It's codependent, but I love her. I pray that she is able to see her family clearly so that she does not resort to food for the days that follow."

"Prayer," wrote Rabbi Harold Kushner in his *When Bad Things Happen to Good People,* "when it is offered in the right way, redeems people from isolation. It assures them that they need not feel alone and abandoned. It lets them know that they are part of a greater reality, with more depth, more hope, more courage, and more of a future than any individual could have by himself."[14]

You *can* make it. With God, you *will* make it. You *will* have the power to act and the strength to persevere. It's a Twelve Step promise.

A LITTLE TORAH FOR THE SOUL
Only the one who brings himself to God as an offering
may be called fully human.

The Rabbi of Rizhyn

INSIGHT FROM OUR TRADITION
For You are Adonai our God,
Who causes the wind to blow and the rain to fall,
For blessing and not for curse,
For life and not for death,
For plenty and not for want.

From the prayers for Shemini Atzeret

SOMETHING TO THINK ABOUT
What is the most important verse in the Bible? "In
all ways, know God" (Proverbs 3:6).

Babylonian Talmud, Berachot 63a

MOVING FROM CODEPENDENCE TO COVENANT
The Koretzer *rebbe* tells a story about a young orphan
boy who inherited only a prayerbook from his parents.
Since he spent his years struggling for personal survival, he was never provided with the opportunity to
learn how to read its Hebrew characters and decipher
its meaning. Utter frustration finally brought him to the
synagogue one *Yom Kippur.* He laid the frail prayerbook in the Holy Ark and shrieked, "Dear God, I do
not know how to pray. Here is the entire prayer book.
Answer its prayers."

A PRAYER FROM THE DEPTHS OF OUR HEARTS
Turn me, *Adonai,* that I may turn.

Lamentations 5:21

Support

Step Twelve

**HAVING HAD A SPIRITUAL AWAKENING
AS A RESULT OF THESE STEPS,
WE TRIED TO CARRY THIS MESSAGE TO OTHER
CO-DEPENDENTS, AND TO PRACTICE THESE PRINCIPLES
IN ALL OUR AFFAIRS**

✓ Finding your spiritual self was a vital part of getting to this point. Recovery awakens the soul and the spirit and life itself is sustained by spiritual renewal.

✓ Working the Twelve Steps—and continuing to work them—brings us closer to our Higher Power and to ourselves.

✓ We begin recovery with self, but continue it with others. Our relationships with people should mirror our loving relationship with God, our Higher Power.

✓ Our recovery can bring wholeness and holiness to everything we do. As we try to bring God into our daily lives in Step Eleven, now we try to bring what we have learned into our lives each day so that we can build a better life for ourselves and better relationships with others.

*E*ven as we continue to work the Steps, for many of us the notion of a spiritual awakening—while we yearn for it—somehow seems beyond our reach. The Twelve Steps remind us that spiritual awakening is possible. So we carry the message with us wherever we go. In whatever we do,

Torah teaches us the way. Here, the sweet wisdom of Rabbi Sheldon Zimmerman, Senior Rabbi of Temple Emanuel in Dallas is instructive. Let his words speak to you as they have to so many others:

> Just *to be* is holy! Just *to be* is holy! Remember, young and old alike, Judaism teaches us that we are free to choose a dozen times a day how we shall react to life's challenges—how to mold ourselves—how to become better than we are. We can't be perfect and some of us are doomed to be always unattractive, but we can be better and kinder and more patient. We can do a few more *mitzvot* and share a few more *simchas* [happy times] and be at one with ourselves, our values and our dreams, our people and our God. You're never too young and you're never too old.
>
> The rabbis asked in the Talmud why one person, Adam, was created. Why, if God wanted to look good, God could have gone SNAP! and you had *Yom Kippur* crowds. God could have done it. Why was only one person created in the Bible first? The Talmud answers that one person was created to teach us that one person is equivalent to a whole world. If you assist one person, you have saved an entire world.
>
> When the days are rushed and you *kvetch* and you don't want to get up, as rotten as things may be, you occupy a time and space in the world and in the universe that no one else occupies. It is yours forever. How you fill it is entirely up to you. No one else can fill it for you. Only you live in that time, and only you live in that space. If you leave it empty, it is empty forever. You have the power to fill that time and space as no one else does. Each step you take, the rabbis teach, leaves its footprints in heaven. You are more than you think you are. You are better than you know. You are capable of doing and being more than you

think you are. You can share your dreams and you can reach them. The purpose of life is to matter, to count, to stand for something, to make a difference.

Lurianic Kabbalah teaches us that when the world was created the sparks scattered in a million directions. You and I are the spark collectors. We possess them and we collect them. We can make God one again. Let us make our gift not truncated days, not days cut short, not days filled with the darkness of depression, but days filled with the sparks of holiness, days filled with making a difference, days filled with simple acts of gentleness, kindness, and love, lived out days—our gift to eternity, our gift to God.

The rabbis were always puzzled about what was actually heard at Sinai. Some said all of Torah was heard. Others said only the *aseret hadibrot,* the ten utterances or Ten Commandments. Maybe only the first statement. Still others suggested that only the first word of the first commandment, *Anochi*—I. Yet, there are those who teach that it was only the first letter of that first word, an *alef,* a silent letter, intensely silent. The spiritual awakening brings with it a different intensity for different people. Thus, God only shares that part of the Divine self that individuals can handle and only when they are ready. One of the reasons we keep going through the Twelve Steps, as throughout our history we have gone through Torah, is that each time we are more ready, more inclined to handle more of the revelation. The Twelve Steps prepare us for the ultimate spiritual renewal, which is only accessible through Torah. In recovery, we continue to recover. That's Twelve Step logic.

Even at this point in your recovery, you may still be uncomfortable calling yourself "codependent." Don't worry about it. The important thing is that you continue your recovery. One way to do it is to share your story at meetings, to qualify, as Twelve Steppers like to say. Share your story of struggle outside the rooms as well. It may be awkward to do so. People may even be taken aback, not used to hearing about an individual's spiritual struggle. But rest assured, they have their own struggle as well. We all do. Carry the message.

One of the major reasons we study sacred text, which is really a history of our people's struggle with faith, is to participate in the faith struggles of our ancestors. Through our engagement with text, those who came before us can help us.

Part of our commitment to Step Twelve is to help others recover, to guide them, nurture them, support them. But to do so within the context of recovery: Ours and theirs.

Moses Maimonides, the *RaMBaM,* taught, "If you see a friend sinning or pursuing an unworthy life, it is a mitzvah to try to restore that person to the right path. Let your friend know that wrong actions are self-inflicted hurts, but speak softly and gently, making it clear that you speak only because of your concern for your friend's well-being."

He was not alone in seeing the need for people to walk life's desert together. That's why we study and pray together, too. Once Menachem Mendl of Kotzk told a "wonder worker" who was versed in the secret act of making a human-like robot that this task was unimportant. What is important, he told the man, is to know the sacred act of making a pious disciple.

This notion of being a student, a disciple, with its implied respect for a teacher is important for our recovery. It helps us to recognize that while we are all individuals, we are linked to one another in a shared tradition, in our shared pursuit of the holy in this world. As we try to practice the principles of recovery in our everyday affairs, we should recall the sage advice of our rabbis: "One who reports a statement of Torah he has heard from someone else should imagine that person standing in front of him as he speaks" (Jerusalem Talmud, *Shabbat* 1:2).

But there is always more to do. Just as we have been helped, we must help others—when we are ready, when they are ready. "Torah begins and ends with loving acts of kindness" (Babylonian Talmud, *Sotah* 14a); whoever gladdens the heart of the unfortunate emulates the presence of God, "reviving the spirit of the humble and reviving the heart of those who are crushed" (Isaiah 57:15).

The rabbis want us to *be Torah,* to be there on the mountaintop of Sinai, to be totally there. To be an example of living a life filled with God's presence, a sacred life. It would be easy to live such a life in isolation, but that's not the Jewish way. Such a life demands action, not withdrawal. The Hebrew word *mitzvot* reflects both God's instruction and our response. They are one in the same.

In the Book of Exodus, we are taught that we are responsible if someone falls into a pit on our property. It is one of the Bible's ways of looking at the responsibility of property ownership—or so we thought. But the Sefas Emes, the rabbi of Ger, said that the pit is one of the Bible's ways of talking about sin. The person who lives a life of loathsome behavior actually digs his own pit. But others may fall into it. Thus, the best way to fill in the hole—and prevent any injury—is through *teshuvah,* a return.

We are all disciples, students of Torah tradition. Come and study. Let's walk to the mountaintop together. And on the way, bring this Twelve Step message of hope to others who may be codependent like you.

Now you're ready to work the Steps—and study Torah—again. It's a perpetual journey, one that raises you closer to Heaven with each step you take.

A LITTLE TORAH FOR THE SOUL
A new word of Torah which comes from the mouth of a repentant person ascends heavenward and adds to the crown of God.

INSIGHT FROM OUR TRADITION
When a person steps down from his bed, that person should say to himself, "Guard your feet when you walk."
Zohar iv, 17b

SOMETHING TO THINK ABOUT

No one is more beloved by God than a messenger sent to perform a good deed who fulfills his errand at the risk of his life.

Bemidbar Rabbah to Numbers 13:1

MOVING FROM CODEPENDENCE TO COVENANT

Of what avail is the mere study of Torah when it is contaminated by pride and temper? The good person should herself be a Torah, and people should be able to learn good conduct from observing her.

Rabbi Leib Saras

A PRAYER FROM THE DEPTHS OF OUR HEARTS

Praised are You, *Adonai* our God, Guide of the Universe, who has kept us alive, preserved us, and helped us to reach this sacred time in our lives.

Shehechiyanu prayer,
said on special occasions

Endnotes

[1] Steinsaltz, Adin, *Teshuvah: A Guide for the Newly Observant Jew* (Free Press, New York, NY, 1987).

[2] Kushner, Lawrence, *God Was In This Place, and I, i Did Not Know* (Jewish Lights Publishing, Woodstock, VT, 1991).

[3] Nachman of Bratzlav, adapted from *Siddur Sim Shalom,* Rabbi Jules Harlow, ed. (The Rabbinical Assembly and the United Synagogue of America, New York, NY, 1985), used with permission.

[4] Klein, A.M., *Hath Not A Jew* (Behrman House, Inc., West Orange, NJ, 1940), used with permission.

[5] Congregation Beth El of the Sudbury River Valley, *Vetaher Lebenu* (Sudbury, MA, 1980), used with permission.

[6] Levy, Richard, ed., *On Wings of Awe* (B'nai B'rith Hillel Foundations, New York, NY, 1985), used with permission.

[7] Kushner, Harold, *When Bad Things Happen to Good People* (Avon, New York, NY, 1983).

[8] Kushner, Lawrence, *Honey from the Rock* (Jewish Lights Publishing, Woodstock, VT, 1990).

[9] Siegel, Danny, *Where Heaven and Earth Touch* (Jason Aronson, Northvale, NJ, 1989).

[10] Friedman, Debbie and Drorah Setel, *"Mi Shebeirach"* Sounds Write Productions, Inc. (ASCAP, 1988), used with permission.

[11] Kushner, Lawrence, *God Was In This Place, and I, i Did Not Know* (Jewish Lights Publishing, Woodstock, VT, 1991).

[12] Dresner, Samuel, *Three Paths of God and Man* (Harper and Brothers, New York, NY, 1960).

[13] Kushner, Lawrence, *God Was In This Place, and I, i Did Not Know* (Jewish Lights Publishing, Woodstock, VT, 1991).

[14] Kushner, Harold, *When Bad Things Happen to Good People* (Avon, New York, NY, 1983).

A Final Blessing

Praised are You, Adonai our God, Guide of the
Universe, who does good to the undeserving
and who has dealt kindly with me.

Birkat Hagomel, blessing of thanks
said after being delivered from mortal danger
or recovering from an illness

Unlocking the Prison of Addiction & Codependence: An Afterword

IN THE SPACE BETWEEN WHO WE ARE AND WHO WE PRETEND TO BE, ADDICTIONS AND CODEPENDENCE TAKE ROOT AND GROW.

Ten years ago I saw an advertisement in the *Los Angeles Times* which read: "Person of Jewish background and culture to work with Jewish criminal offenders. M.S.W. required." My spirit soared. The hairs on my arms stood up. In my heart, I knew that this was my calling. I had been yearning for it, but had never found it. I couldn't wait to tell my family. They'd never believe it. Jewish criminals indeed!

I was originally hired by Gateways Hospital and Mental Health Center as a field representative with the Jewish Committee for Personal Service, a seventy-year-old agency concerned with Jews in jails and prisons.

My first client at Sybil Brand County Jail for Women in Los Angeles was a woman my age, a college graduate who was also a high school English teacher. Her daughter already grown, this woman was about to become a grandmother. She was also a heroin addict who had been arrested for selling drugs. The strong connection we established that day literally transformed both of us. She began the process of recovery and I was committed to helping addicts find the road to spiritual renewal through recovery. For the first time, the words "there but for the Grace of God go I" had a profound sense of meaning.

Only a few days later, I received a call from a distraught mother. She had just hung up the phone after a tearful conversation with her daughter. The girl was in jail, begging her parents to bail her out, telling tales of anti-Semitic epithets by guards and assaults by fellow inmates. This codependent mother was tormented by guilt and fear: "I called the police and had her arrested to save her life," she sobbed. "If I bail her out, she'll kill herself with cocaine." She knew she was acting out of love, "tough love," we call it, but she felt like a monster nonetheless. When I later visited the daughter in jail, I explained her family's decision not to bail her out. She was bitter, outraged: "How could they do this to their own flesh and blood?" To her, their intention was punitive and vengeful: "You couldn't love your daughter and lock her up." I am both a daughter and a mother; I felt the pain of each. Slowly, I began to realize how addiction impacts every family member. It is, in fact, a family disease.

Addicts compulsively chase drugs, alcohol, food, gambling, money, sex, or excitement in order to "fix" themselves. The codependent members of the family compulsively conspire to "fix" the addict. Over the last ten years I have known hundreds of addicted families caught in the web of codependency. They cajole, control, bribe, blame, and manipulate one another. The addict lies and the codependent families believe him. She promises and they trust her. He steals from them and they forgive him. They threaten to stop taking care of her and he tells them that he has no food in the house. "How will it help him to go hungry?" a mother asks plaintively. These parents who have been brought up to express love by giving everything, who expected their children to reward them by becoming successful, are completely baffled. "He could have had anything he wanted. He had such potential. How could he throw his life away?" They have been conditioned to believe that with enough money and enough expertise, they can repair anything. They obsessively seek solutions to *his or her* problem, provide whatever he tells them will make him feel better. They buy for him. They beg for her to get help and borrow money to pay for her treatment. The more they give, the more he feels entitled to receive. The more they "enable," the less responsibility she accepts for the consequences of her actions. They are hooked together by their shared belief that his addiction is their failure, their shame.

These addicted, codependent families are not aberrations. They are Jewish—Reform, Conservative, Orthodox and Reconstructionist—Christian and secular. They are unaffiliated and affiliated, educated and uneducated. They are sons and daughters, mothers, fathers, grandmothers and grandfathers. They are doctors, lawyers, accountants, carpenters, psychiatrists, and even rabbis. In other words, *they are us* and we are them.

Codependence reflects our fragmentation of spirit. All of our "golden calves" and "graven images" have failed to fill the void at the center of our being. In my opinion, codependence is the result of our lack of authenticity. It is the substitution of image for self. We don't walk our talk. What's in our hearts is not on our lips. Our inner and outer selves don't match. Rhetoric and reality are light-years apart. We put form before substance, prefer appearances to truth. We role-play our intimate relationships, hiding our true selves for fear of ridicule or rejection. "We spend money we don't have to buy things we don't need to impress people we don't like." Parents who need the approval of "the neighbors," who judge themselves and others by the accomplishments of their children, attempt to control their children and make them perfect. Children who need their parents' approval either accept the control and conform, or reject it and rebel. Neither is freedom. Neither allows for authenticity. In the space between who we are and who we pretend to be, addictions and codependence take root and grow.

Recovery from codependence requires an acceptance that one is powerless over other people, that one cannot control the outcomes of events. It means that self-validation comes as a by-product of service and serenity comes from the surrender of the individual will to God's will. Codependence is our modern *Mitzrayim* (our Egypt) and we are searching for a way out of the wilderness, back to ourselves, back to our Jewish roots: An example and model for people of other faiths, too.

An ever-increasing number of Jewish addicts and their codependents are experiencing in their recovery a spiritual reawakening through Twelve Step programs. They are hungry for God in their lives and look to Judaism to nourish them. Thanks to Rabbi Kerry Olitzky and Jewish Lights Publishing, we now have a body of literature which integrates Judaism and Twelve Step recovery.

Rabbi Olitzky and Jewish Lights Publishing have profoundly impacted the Jewish recovery movement. When we opened Gateways Beit T'Shuvah five years ago to help addicts on parole recover from their addiction and help their codependent families, as well, I thought that integrating Judaism and the Twelve Steps was a somewhat heretical idea. There was no body of literature to support it. It was a lone article by Abraham Twerski, entitled "Judaism and the Twelve Steps," which really gave me the courage to persevere. This led me to the JACS (Jewish Alcoholics, Chemically Dependent and Significant Others) Foundation in New York City and a thick reference book called *Addictions in the Jewish Community*, published by the Federation of Jewish Philanthropies in New York. But when *Twelve Jewish Steps to Recovery* was published I was ecstatic. I am equally excited about *Renewed Each Day: Daily Twelve Step Recovery Meditations Based on the Bible* and this book, *Recovery from Codependence: A Jewish Twelve Steps Guide to Healing Your Soul*. I use them all to help our residents, their families, staff members, and our board of directors.

Thank you Rabbi Olitzky and Jewish Lights Publishing for giving the Jewish recovery movement the voice and visibility we need to be acknowledged and accepted by the Jewish community.

HARRIET ROSSETTO
*Director, Jewish Committee
for Personal Service
Founder, Gateways Beit T'shuvah*

The Twelve Steps of Alcoholics Anonymous

The Twelve Steps are reprinted and adapted with permission of Alcoholics Anonymous World Services, Inc. Permission to reprint and adapt the Twelve Steps does not mean that A.A. is affiliated with the program. A.A. is a program of recovery from alcoholism—use of the Twelve Steps in connection with programs and activities which are patterned after A.A. but which address other problems does not imply otherwise.

1. We admitted we were powerless over alcohol—that our lives had become unmanageable.

2. Came to believe that a Power greater than ourselves could restore us to sanity.

3. Made a decision to turn our will and our lives over to the care of God as we understood Him.

4. Made a searching and fearless inventory of ourselves.

5. Admitted to God, to ourselves, and to another human being the exact nature of our wrongs.

6. Were entirely ready to have God remove all these defects of character.

7. Humbly asked Him to remove our shortcomings.

8. Made a list of all persons we had harmed, and became willing to make amends to them all.

9. Made dircct amends to such people wherever possible, except when to do so would injure them or others.

10. Continued to take personal inventory and when we were wrong promptly admitted it.

11. Sought through prayer and meditation to improve our conscious contact with God as we understood Him, praying only for knowledge of His will for us and the power to carry that out.

12. Having had a spiritual awakening as a result of these Steps, we tried to carry this message to alcoholics, and to practice these principles in all our affairs.

(The use of the masculine pronoun in referring to God is the original A.A. language. Like many Twelve Step programs, we have chosen not to use a pronoun at all in our discussion, but retain the original here.)

The Twelve Traditions
of
Alcoholics Anonymous

The Twelve Traditions are reprinted and adapted with permission of Alcoholics Anonymous World Services, Inc. Permission to reprint and adapt the Twelve Traditions does not mean that A.A. is affiliated with the program. A.A. is a program of recovery from alcoholism— use of the Twelve Traditions in connection with programs and activities which are patterned after A.A. but which address other problems does not imply otherwise.

1. Our common welfare should come first; personal recovery depends upon A.A. unity.

2. For our group purpose there is but one ultimate authority—a loving God as He may express Himself in our group conscience. Our leaders are but trusted servants; they do not govern.

3. The only requirement for A.A. membership is a desire to stop drinking.

4. Each group should be autonomous except in matters affecting other groups or A.A. as a whole.

5. Each group has but one primary purpose—to carry its message to the alcoholic who still suffers.

6. An A.A. group ought never endorse, finance, or lend the A.A. name to any related facility or outside enterprise lest problems of money, property, and prestige divert us from our primary purpose.

7. Every A.A. group ought to be fully self-supporting, declining outside contributions.

8. Alcoholics Anonymous should remain forever non-professional, but our service centers may employ special workers.

9. A.A., as such, ought never be organized; but we may create service boards or committees directly responsible to those they serve.

10. Alcoholics Anonymous has no opinion on outside issues; hence the A.A. name ought never be drawn into public controversy.

11. Our public relations policy is based on attraction rather than promotion; we need always maintain personal anonymity at the level of press, radio, and film.

12. Anonymity is the spiritual foundation of all our traditions, ever reminding us to place principles before personality.

(The use of the masculine pronoun in referring to God is the original A.A. language. Like many Twelve Step programs, we have chosen not to use a pronoun at all in our discussion, but retain the original here.)

For Further Help

(and to find a local group in your community)

Al-Anon Family Groups, Inc.
1372 Broadway
New York, NY 10018
212/ 302-7240

Alateen
1372 Broadway
New York, NY 10018
212/ 302-7240

Alcoholics Anonymous World Services, Inc. (A.A.)
G.S.O.
Grand Central Sta.
Box 459
New York, NY 10163
212/ 870-3400

Cocaine Anonymous (CA)
World Services Offices
3740 Overland Avenue,
Suite H
Los Angeles, CA 90034
310/ 559-5833
800/ 347-8998

Co-Dependents Anonymous (CoDA)
P.O. Box 33577
Phoenix, AZ 85067-3577
602/ 277-7991

Codependents of Sex Addicts Anonymous (CoSA)
P.O. Box 14537
Minneapolis, MN 55414
612/ 537-6904

Debtors Anonymous
P.O. Box 20322
New York, NY 10025
212/ 642-8222

Dentists Concerned for Dentists
450 N. Syndicate, Suite 117
St. Paul, MN 55104
612/ 641-0730

Divorce Anonymous
2600 Colorado Avenue,
Suite 270
Santa Monica, CA 90404
310/ 998-6538

Drugs Anonymous (DA)
(Pills Anonymous)
P.O. Box 473
Ansonia Station
New York, NY 10023
212/ 874-0700

Emotional Health Anonymous
2420 San Gabriel Blvd.
Rosemead, CA 91770
818/ 240-3215

Emotions Anonymous
P.O. Box 4245
St. Paul, MN 55104
612/ 647-9712

Families Anonymous
P.O. Box 528
Van Nuys, CA 91408
818/ 989-7841
800/ 736-9805

Families of Sex Offenders Anonymous
152 West Walk
W. Haven, CT 06516
203/ 931-0015

Gam-Anon Family Groups
P.O. Box 157
Whitestone, NY 11357
718/ 352-1671

Gamblers Anonymous
P.O. Box 17173
Los Angeles, CA 90017
213/ 386-8789

GROW
(for those with emotional breakdowns)
P.O. Box 3667
Champaign, IL 61826
217/ 352-6989

Homosexuals Anonymous
H.A. Fellowship Services
P.O. Box 7881
Reading, PA 19603
215/ 376-1146

HIVIES
(HIV and substance abusers)
610 Greenwood
Glenview, IL
708/ 724-3832

JACS Foundation
(Jewish Alcoholics, Chemically Dependent Persons and Significant Others)
426 West 58th Street
New York, NY 10019
212/ 397-4197

Nar-Anon
P.O. Box 2562
Palos Verdes, CA 90274
310/ 547-5800

Narcotics Anonymous (NA)
World Services Office
P.O. Box 9999
Van Nuys, CA 91409
818/ 780-3951

National Council on Alcoholism and Drug Dependence (NCADD)
12 West 21st Street
New York, NY 10010
800/ NCA-CALL

National Self-Help Clearinghouse
25 West 43rd Street
Room 620
New York, NY 10036
212/ 642-2944

Nicotine Anonymous
2118 Greenwich Street
San Francisco, CA 94123
415/ 922-8575

O-Anon
(family and friends of
compulsive overeaters)
P.O. Box 748
San Pedro, CA 90733
310/ 547-1570

**Obsessive Compulsive
Anonymous**
P.O. Box 215
New Hyde Park, NY
11040
516/ 741-4901

Overeaters Anonymous
117 West 26th Street,
Room 2W
New York, NY 10001
212/ 206-8621

Parents Anonymous
520 S. La Fayette Park
Place, Suite 316
Los Angeles, CA 90057
800/ 775-1134

Pill Addicts Anonymous
P.O. Box 273
Reading, PA 19603
215/ 372-1128

Recoveries Anonymous
P.O. Box 1212
Hewitt Square Station
East Northport, NY 11731
516/ 261-1212

S-Anon
(family and friends of sex
addicts)
P.O. Box 5117
Sherman Oaks, CA 91413
818/ 990-6910

**Schizophrenics
Anonymous**
15920 W. Twelve Mile Rd.
Southfield, MI 48076
313/ 477-1983

Sex Addicts Anonymous
P.O. Box 3038
Minneapolis, MN 55403
612/ 339-0217

Sexaholics Anonymous
P.O. Box 300
Simi Valley, CA 93062
818/ 704-9854

**Sex and Love Addicts
Anonymous**
P.O. Box 119
New Town Branch
Boston, MA 02258
617/ 332-1845

**Sexual Compulsives
Anonymous**
(East Coast)
P.O. Box 1585
Old Chelsea Station
New York, NY 10011
212/ 439-1123

**Sexual Compulsives
Anonymous**
(West Coast)
4391 Sunset Boulevard
Suite 520
Los Angeles, CA 90029
213/ 859-5585

**Survivors of Incest
Anonymous**
P.O. Box 21817
Baltimore, MD 21222
301/ 282-3400

**Unwed Parents Anony-
mous**
P.O. Box 44556
Phoenix, AR 85064
602/ 952-1463

**Women Helping
Divorced Women**
543 N. Fairfax Avenue
Santa Monica, CA 90036
310/ 998-6538

Women for Sobriety
P.O. Box 618
Quakertown, PA 18951
800/ 333-1606

**Workaholics
Anonymous**
P.O. Box 661501
Los Angeles, CA 90066
310/ 859-5804

Glossary of Important Words & Concepts

Adonai: God is known by various names in Jewish tradition. Adonai (literally "Lord") is used to refer to God since we do not know how to (and dare not) pronounce God's essential name

cheshbon hanefesh: a probing inventory of the soul, taken by individuals throughout the year but most especially prior to the High Holy Days

codependence: You may be a codependent person if you are in a relationship with an alcoholic or addicted person, someone who has an eating disorder, engages in compulsive gambling or sex, if you are addicted to a relationship or if you live in a dysfunctional family

covenant: the agreement established some 3,200 years ago between God and the people of Israel at Sinai

Elul: the month prior to the High Holy Days (usually middle to late August to early to mid-September), which focuses on introspection, repentance, and renewal

kavannah: literally, the intention with which you do something; while technically the term is used to refer to all unfixed prayers, it also reflects those texts which when chanted repetitively prepare the individual for prayer

midbar: literally the desert, a place of emotional emptiness

mishkan: the portable desert sanctuary

mitzvah (pl. mitzvot): divine commandments, holy instructions, given by God to the Jewish people. It also

121

reflects the individual response to this Divine direction. Also sometimes used to mean "A good deed."

selichot: prayers of penitence, recited particularly prior to the High Holy Days

Shechinah: God's presence

shelemut (shalom): wholeness and completeness, serenity, epitomized by peace

teshuvah: literally a turning toward God and to a righteous, religious way of life; in a broader sense, this represents returning and moving forward in recovery

yetzer hara: the inclination to do evil; more broadly, one's inner drives

yetzer tov: the inner drive to do good

Yom Kippur: Day of Atonement; according to many the holiest day of the year, this holy day is called the Sabbath of Sabbaths. More than any other time on the Jewish calendar, it epitomizes the focus on introspection, repentance, and personal renewal.

Selected Readings

The Book of Psalms: A New Translation
Jewish Publication Society
Philadelphia, Pennsylvania

Four Centuries of Jewish Women's Spirituality: A Sourcebook
Ed. Ellen M. Umansky and Dianne Ashton
Beacon Press
Boston, Massachusetts

God Was In This Place and I, i Did Not Know
Lawrence Kushner
Jewish Lights Publishing
Woodstock, Vermont

Growing Each Day
Abraham J. Twerski
Mesorah Publications
New York, New York

To Grow in Wisdom: An Anthology of Abraham Joshua Heschel
Ed. Jacob Neusner
Modern Books
New York, New York

The Heavenly Ladder: The Jewish Guide to Inner Growth
Edward Hoffman
Harper and Row
San Francisco, California

Honey from the Rock: An Introduction to Jewish Mysticism
Lawrence Kushner
Jewish Lights Publishing
Woodstock, Vermont

I Didn't Ask To Be in This Family
Abraham Twerski
St. Martin's Press
New York, New York

The Lights of Penitence
Abraham Isaac Kook,
Trans. Ben Zion Bokser
Paulist Press
Mahwah, New Jersey

Living Each Day
Abraham J. Twerski
Mesorah Publications
New York, New York

Out of the Depths I Call to You: A Book of Prayers for the Married Jewish Woman
Ed. Nina Beth Cardin
Jason Aronson, Inc.
Northvale, New Jersey

Pirke Avot: A New Translation and Commentary
Leonard Kravitz and Kerry Olitzky
Union of American Hebrew Congregations
New York, New York

Renewed Each Day: Daily Twelve Step Recovery Meditations Based on the Bible (2 vols.)
Kerry Olitzky and Aaron Z.
Jewish Lights Publishing
Woodstock, Vermont

The Sabbath
Abraham Joshua Heschel
Farrar, Straus, and Giroux
New York, New York

Self-Discovery in Recovery
Abraham J. Twerski
Hazelden Educational
Materials
Center City, Minnesota

Teshuvah: A Guide for the Newly Observant Jew
Adin Steinsaltz ,
Trans. Michael Swirsky
Free Press
New York, New York

This is the Path: Twelve Step Programs in a Jewish Context
Rami Shapiro
EnR Wordsmiths
Miami, Florida

Twelve Jewish Steps To Recovery: A Personal Guide to Turning From Alcoholism and Other Addictions
Kerry Olitzky and
Stuart Copans
Jewish Lights Publishing
Woodstock, Vermont

The Twelve Steps and the Jewish Tradition
Susan Berman
Hazelden Educational
Materials
Center City, Minnesota

Waking Up Just in Time
Abraham J. Twerski
Pharos Books
New York, New York

When Do the Good Things Start?
Abraham J. Twerski
St. Martin's Press
New York, New York

About Us

RABBI KERRY M. OLITZKY, D.H.L., is director of the School of Education at Hebrew Union College-Jewish Institute of Religion, New York and directs its graduate studies program. He has been a leader in developing training programs for clergy of all faiths, especially in the area of addiction and codependence. A pioneer in the field of pastoral care and counseling in the Jewish community, he writes and lectures widely on topics related to spiritual renewal.

Rabbi Olitzky is co-author of *Renewed Each Day: Daily Twelve Step Recovery Meditations Based on the Bible* (Jewish Lights Publishing, 1992); *Twelve Jewish Steps To Recovery: A Personal Guide to Turning From Alcoholism and Other Addictions* (Jewish Lights Publishing, 1991) and is currently at work on *One Hundred Blessings Every Day: Daily Twelve Step Recovery Meditations* (Jewish Lights Publishing, 1993), a book of daily meditations and affirmations based on the calendar and holiday cycle.

He is producer and moderator of "Message of Israel" (ABC Radio Network) and annual special issue editor on aging and Judaism for the *Journal of Psychology and Judaism*.

MARC GALANTER, M.D. is Professor of Psychiatry and Director, Division of Alcoholism and Drug Abuse, New York University Medical Center, New York, New York. He is the author of *Network Therapy for Alcohol and Drug Abuse: A New Approach in Practice* (Basic Books, 1993).

HARRIET ROSSETTO, L.C.S.W. is director of the Jewish Committee for Personal Service and founder of Gateways Beit T'Shuvah in Los Angeles. Gateways Beit T'Shuvah is a halfway house for Jewish addicts and offenders that is based on Twelve Step programs and the spiritual principles of Judaism. She is presently working on a book about families of addicts and the institutions in the Jewish community which serve them.

About the Illustrations

Artist **MATY GRÜNBERG**'s illustration of the Zion gate of the Old City of Jerusalem opens each chapter of *Recovery from Codependence* as the reader is welcomed into another Jewish Twelve Steps experience. It was selected to emphasize the relationship between heavenly and earthly in all our lives through the prism of Jerusalem.

One enters a different plane of reality both physically and spiritually when entering the gates of the Old City. Our lives were changed by Jerusalem. We invited Maty Grünberg to draw the gates of his beloved city for the publication of *Twelve Jewish Steps to Recovery: A Personal Guide to Turning from Alcoholism and Other Addictions*, by Rabbi Kerry M. Olitzky and Stuart A. Copans, M.D. Recognizing that Jerusalem is the center of the Jewish and Christian spiritual worlds, we reproduce this gate so that you might enter it also, one step at a time.

About JEWISH LIGHTS Publishing

People of all faiths and backgrounds yearn for books that attract, engage, educate and spiritually inspire.

Our principal goal is to stimulate thought and help all people learn about who the Jewish People are, where they come from, and what the future can be made to hold. While people of our diverse Jewish heritage are the primary audience, our books speak to the Christian world as well and will broaden their understanding of Judaism and the roots of their own faith.

We bring to you authors who are at the forefront of spiritual thought and experience. While each has something different to say, they all say it in a voice that you can hear.

Our books are designed to welcome you and then to engage, stimulate and inspire. We judge our success not only by whether or not our books are beautiful and commercially successful, but by whether or not they make a difference in your life.

We at Jewish Lights take great care to produce beautiful books that present meaningful spiritual content in a form that reflects the art of making high quality books. Therefore, we want to acknowledge those who contributed to the production of this book.

ART DIRECTION AND PRODUCTION
Rachel Kahn

TYPE:
Set in Garamond and Mistral
Barbara Homeyer Type, Lebanon, NH

COVER PRINTING
Phoenix Color, Long Island City, NY

PRINTING AND BINDING
Book Press, Inc., Brattleboro, VT

Spiritual Inspiration for Daily Living

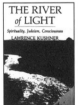

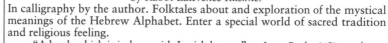

AWARD WINNER

THE BOOK OF LETTERS
A Mystical Hebrew Alphabet
by *Rabbi Lawrence Kushner*

In calligraphy by the author. Folktales about and exploration of the mystical meanings of the Hebrew Alphabet. Enter a special world of sacred tradition and religious feeling.

"A book which is in love with Jewish letters." — *Isaac Bashevis Singer*

• **Popular Hardcover Edition**
6"x 9", 80 pp. Hardcover, two colors, inspiring new Foreword.
ISBN 1-879045-00-1 **$24.95**

• **Deluxe Presentation Edition**
9"x 12", 80 pp. Hardcover, four-color text, ornamentation, in a beautiful slipcase.
ISBN 1-879045-01-X **$79.95**

• **Collector's Limited Edition**
9"x 12", 80 pp. Hardcover, gold embossed pages, hand assembled slipcase. With silkscreened print.
Limited to 500 signed and numbered copies.
ISBN 1-879045-04-4 **$349.00**

AWARD WINNER # THE SPIRIT OF RENEWAL
Crisis & Response in Jewish Life
by *Edward Feld*

"Boldly redefines the landscape of Jewish religious thought after the Holocaust."
— *Rabbi Lawrence Kushner*

In order to address the question of faith after the Holocaust, Rabbi Feld explores three key cycles of destruction and recovery in Jewish history, each of which radically reshaped Jewish understanding of God, people, and the world.

"Undoubtedly the most moving book I have read....'Must' reading." — *Rabbi Howard A. Addison,*
Conservative Judaism

6"x 9", 208 pp. Hardcover, ISBN 1-879045-06-0 **$22.95**

MOURNING & MITZVAH
A Guided Journal for Walking the Mourner's Path Through Grief to Healing
• WITH OVER 60 GUIDED EXERCISES •   by *Anne Brener, L.C.S.W.*

"Fully engaging in mourning means you will be a different person than before you began."
For those who mourn a death, for those who would help them, for those who face a loss of any kind.
"A stunning book! It offers an exploration in depth of the place where psychology and religious ritual intersect, and the name of that place is Truth."
—*Rabbi Harold Kushner, author of* When Bad Things Happen to Good People
6" x 9", 272 pp. Quality Paperback, ISBN 1-879045-23-0 **$19.95**

PUTTING GOD ON THE GUEST LIST
How to Reclaim the Spiritual Meaning of Your Child's Bar or Bat Mitzvah
by *Rabbi Jeffrey K. Salkin*
Foreword by *Rabbi Sandy Eisenberg Sasso*
Introduction by *Rabbi William H. Lebeau, Vice Chancellor, JTS*
Joining explanation, instruction and inspiration, helps parent and child truly *be there* when the moment of Sinai is recreated in their lives. Asks and answers such fundamental questions as how did Bar and Bat Mitzvah originate? What is the lasting significance of the event? How to make the event more spiritually meaningful?
"Shows the way to restore spirituality and depth to every young Jew's most important rite of passsage."
— *Rabbi Joseph Telushkin, author of* Jewish Literacy
"As a Catholic clergyman who has helped prepare young people for confirmation, I find Rabbi Salkin's book to be a source of inspiration and direction." — *Msgr. Thomas Hartman, co-host, "The God Squad."*

6"x 9", 184 pp. Hardcover, ISBN 1-879045-20-6 **$21.95**
6"x 9", 184 pp. Quality Paperback, ISBN 1-879045-10-9 **$14.95**

Add Greater Understanding to Your Life

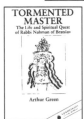

Motivation, Inspiration
& Consolation for Recovery

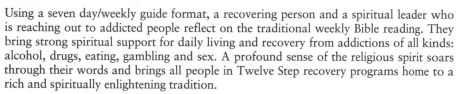

RENEWED EACH DAY
Daily Twelve Step Recovery Meditations
Based on the Bible
by *Rabbi Kerry M. Olitzky & Aaron Z.*
VOLUME I: Genesis & Exodus
Introduction by *Rabbi Michael A. Signer*
Afterword by JACS Foundation
VOLUME II: Leviticus, Numbers & Deuteronomy
Introduction by *Sharon M. Strassfeld*
Afterword by *Rabbi Harold M. Schulweis*

Using a seven day/weekly guide format, a recovering person and a spiritual leader who is reaching out to addicted people reflect on the traditional weekly Bible reading. They bring strong spiritual support for daily living and recovery from addictions of all kinds: alcohol, drugs, eating, gambling and sex. A profound sense of the religious spirit soars through their words and brings all people in Twelve Step recovery programs home to a rich and spiritually enlightening tradition.

"Meets a vital need; it offers a chance for people turning from alcoholism and addiction to renew their spirits and draw upon the Jewish tradition to guide and enrich their lives."
—*Rabbi Irving (Yitz) Greenberg, President, CLAL,*
The National Jewish Center for Learning and Leadership

"Will benefit anyone familiar with a 'religion of the Book.' Jews, Christians, Muslims. . . ."
—*Ernest Kurtz, author of* Not-God: A History of Alcoholics
Anonymous *&* The Spirituality of Imperfection

"An enduring impact upon the faith community as it seeks to blend the wisdom of the ages represented in the tradition with the twelve steps to recovery and wholeness."
—*Robert H. Albers, Ph.D., Editor,* Journal of Ministry in Addiction & Recovery

Beautiful Two-Volume Set.
6"x 9", V. I, 224 pp. / V. II, 280 pp., Quality Paperback, ISBN 1-879045-21-4   **$27.90**

Recovery from
Codependence

A Jewish
Twelve Steps
Guide to
Healing
Your Soul

RECOVERY FROM CODEPENDENCE
A Jewish Twelve Steps Guide to Healing Your Soul
 by *Rabbi Kerry M. Olitzky*
Foreword by *Marc Galanter, M.D., Director,*
Division of Alcoholism & Drug Abuse, NYU Medical Center
Afterword by *Harriet Rosetto, Director, Gateways Beit T'shuvah*
For the estimated 90% of America struggling with the addiction of a family member or loved one, or involved in a dysfunctional family or relationship. A follow-up to the ground-breaking *Twelve Jewish Steps to Recovery.*

"The disease of chemical dependency is also a family illness. Rabbi Olitzky offers spiritual hope and support." —*Jerry Spicer, President, Hazelden*

"Another major step forward in finding the sources and resources of healing, both physical and spiritual, in our tradition." —*Rabbi Sheldon Zimmerman, Temple Emanu-El, Dallas, TX*

6" x 9", 160 pp. Hardcover, ISBN 1-879045-27-3 **$21.95**
6" x 9", 160 pp. Quality Paperback, ISBN 1-879045-32-X **$13.95**

Twelve Jewish Steps To Recovery

A Personal Guide To Turning From Alcoholism & Other Addictions....Drugs, Food, Gambling, Sex

by *Rabbi Kerry M. Olitzky & Stuart A. Copans, M.D.*
Preface by Abraham J. Twerski, M.D.
Introduction by Rabbi Sheldon Zimmerman
Illustrations by Maty Grünberg
"Getting Help" by JACS Foundation
A Jewish perspective on the Twelve Steps of addiction recovery programs with consolation, inspiration and motivation for recovery. It draws from traditional sources, and quotes from what recovering Jewish people say about their experiences with addictions of all kinds. Inspiring illustrations of the twelve gates of the Old City of Jerusalem.

This book is not just for Jewish people.

It's for all people who would gain strength to heal and insight from Jewish tradition.

- All people who are in trouble with alcohol and drugs and other addictions — food, gambling, sex
- Anyone seeking an understanding of the Twelve Steps from a Jewish perspective — regardless of religious background or affiliation
- Alcoholics and addicts in recovery
- Codependents
- Adult children of alcoholics
- Specialists in recovery and treatment

Experts Praise *Twelve Jewish Steps To Recovery*

"Recommended reading for people of all denominations." — Rabbi Abraham J. Twerski, M.D.

"I read Twelve Jewish Steps with the eyes of a Christian and came away renewed in my heart. I felt like I had visited my Jewish roots. These authors have deep knowledge of recovery as viewed by Alcoholics Anonymous." — Rock J. Stack, M.A., L.L.D. Manager of Clinical/Pastoral Education, Hazelden Foundation

"This book is the first aimed directly at helping the addicted person and family. Everyone affected or interested should read it." — Sheila B. Blume, M.D., C.A.C., Medical Director, Alcoholism, Chemical Dependency and Compulsive Gambling Programs, South Oaks Hospital, Amityville, NY

Readers Praise *Twelve Jewish Steps To Recovery*

"A God-send. Literally. A book from the higher power." — New York, NY
"Looking forward to using it in my practice." —Michigan City, IN
"No words can describe my gratitude." — Chicago, IL
"Made me feel as though 12 Steps were for me, too." — Long Beach, CA
"Inspiring and reassuring." — Pomona, NJ
"Spiritual, sensitive, realistic, helpful." — Tallahassee, FL
"Excellent–changed my life." — Elkhart Lake, WI
"Traditionally Jewish and helpful!" — Monsey, NY

6" x 9", 136 pp. Hardcover, ISBN 1-879045-08-7 **$19.95**
6" x 9", 136 pp. Quality Paperback, ISBN 1-879045-09-5 **$12.95**

Order Information

Please send me the following book(s):

• *Motivation & Inspiration for Recovery* •

_____	Recovery From Codependence, (hc) $21.95 _____
_____	Recovery From Codependence, (pb) $13.95 _____
_____	Renewed Each Day, 2-Volume Set, (pb) $27.90 _____
_____	Twelve Jewish Steps To Recovery, (hc) $19.95 _____
_____	Twelve Jewish Steps To Recovery, (pb) $12.95 _____

_____ The Jerusalem Gates Portfolio, (all 12 prints), $49.95 *50% Savings* _____

_____ The Jerusalem Gates Portfolio, Any 3 prints $25.

List numbers here: _____ _____ _____

• *Other Inspiring Books* •

_____ Aspects Of Rabbinic Theology, (pb) $18.95 _____

The Book Of Letters

_____ • Popular Hardcover Edition, $24.95 _____

_____ • Deluxe Presentation Edition w/ slipcase, $79.95, *plus* $5.95 s/h _____

_____ • Collector's Limited Edition, $349.00, *plus* $12.95 s/h _____

_____ God's Paintbrush, (hc) $15.95 _____

_____ God Was In This Place And I, i Did Not Know, (hc) $21.95 _____

_____ God Was In This Place And I, i Did Not Know, (pb) $16.95 _____

_____ Honey From The Rock, (pb) $14.95 _____

_____ The Last Trial, (pb) $16.95 _____

_____ Mourning & Mitzvah, (pb) $19.95 _____

_____ Putting God On The Guest List, (hc) $21.95 _____

_____ Putting God On The Guest List, (pb) $14.95 _____

_____ The River Of Light, (pb) $14.95 _____

_____ Seeking The Path To Life, (hc) $19.95 _____

_____ So That Your Values Live On, (hc) $23.95 _____

_____ So That Your Values Live On, (pb) $16.95 _____

_____ Spirit Of Renewal, (hc) $22.95 _____

_____ Tormented Master, (pb) $17.95 _____

_____ Your Word Is Fire, (pb) $14.95 *Available June 1993* _____

For s/h, add $2.95 for the first book, $1 each additional book. _____

Total _____

Check enclosed for $ _____ *payable to:* JEWISH LIGHTS Publishing.

Charge my credit card: ❏ MasterCard ❏ Visa ❏ Discover ❏ AMEX

Credit Card # _____ Expires _____

Name on card _____

Signature _____ Phone ( ) _____

Name _____

Street _____

City / State / Zip _____

Phone or mail to: JEWISH LIGHTS Publishing

Box 237, Sunset Farm Offices, Route 4, Woodstock, Vermont 05091

Tel (802) 457-4000   *Fax* (802) 457-4004

Toll free credit card orders (800) 962-4544 (9AM–5PM EST Monday–Friday)

Generous discounts on quantity orders. SATISFACTION GUARANTEED. Prices subject to change.

Available from better bookstores. Try your bookstore first.